Andrew Byers

faith
without
illusions

following Jesus as a cynic-saint

IVP Books

An imprint of InterVarsity Press
Downers Grove, Illinois

InterVarsity Press
P.O. Box 1400, Downers Grove, IL 60515-1426
World Wide Web: www.ivpress.com
Email: email@ivpress.com

InterVarsity Press® is the book-publishing division of InterVarsity Christian Fellowship/USA®, a movement of students and faculty active on campus at hundreds of universities, colleges and schools of nursing in the United States of America, and a member movement of the International Fellowship of Evangelical Students. For information about local and regional activities, write Public Relations Dept., InterVarsity Christian Fellowship/USA, 6400 Schroeder Rd., P.O. Box 7895, Madison, WI 53707-7895, or visit the IVCF website at <www.intervarsity.org>.

All Scripture quotations, unless otherwise indicated, are taken from the Holy Bible, English Standard Version®. ESV®. Copyright ©2001 by Crossway Bibles, a division of Good News Publishers. Used by permission. All rights reserved.

Design: Cindy Kiple
Images: Yosemite chapel: Jason Woodcock/iStockphoto
           man walking away: Renee Keith/iStockphoto

ISBN 978-0-8308-3618-5

Printed in Canada ∞

 InterVarsity Press is committed to protecting the environment and to the responsible use of natural resources. As a member of Green Press Initiative we use recycled paper whenever possible. To learn more about the Green Press Initiative, visit <www .greenpressinitiative.org>.

Library of Congress Cataloging-in-Publication Data

Byers, Andrew J., 1974-
  Faith without illusions: following Jesus as a cynic saint / Andrew
J. Byers.
     p. cm.
  Includes bibliographical references.
  ISBN 978-0-8308-3618-5 (pbk.: alk paper)
  1. Christianity—Psychology. 2. Cynicism. I. Title.
  BR110.B94 2010
  234'.2—dc22

                                                          2010040609

P 18 17 16 15 14 13 12 11 10 9 8 7 6 5 4 3 2 1

Y 25 24 23 22 21 20 19 18 17 16 15 14 13 12 11

contents

1

cynical
between
the edens

Heard a sneer outside the garden
Salutation so well-heeled
Welcome all you suckers to
Struggleville

—Bill Mallonee, "Welcome to Struggleville"

He who loves his dream of a community more than the
Christian community itself becomes a destroyer of the latter, even
though his personal intentions may be ever so honest and earnest and
sacrificial.

—Dietrich Bonhoeffer, *Life Together*

FALLING

Most of us do not actively seek to embrace cynicism. We fall into it.

I fell rather hard in the sixth grade.

It was 1986. That was the first year we had lockers, and their metallic clang and bang added a new hallway sound. Vocab quizzes replaced the elementary spelling tests, but most of the new words in our mouths were of the "dirty" variety, and we whispered them awkwardly for laughs and furtively wrote them on our desks in #2 graph-

ite. Newly awakened hormones spawned a feral hallway energy distinctively unlike that of the fifth grade hall. Cliques of "cool" and
"uncool" were beginning to solidify. You could almost smell the pun-
gent aura of territorialism in the halls between each class. It was the
last year of outdoor recess. It was the year Wanda Turner had a "period" (whatever that was). It was the year when the boys *and* the girls
were taller than I. It was my first experience of corporal punishment
in the school system. It was the worst year of my life.

And in that year I fell in love.

She and I were good friends, but she was in love with *him*. You
know the one: the guy who had a bit of height on him, no acne and
that roguish charm that girls find so irresistible. The role of quarter-
back was given to him without dispute for every football game at recess. When a girl became "It" in freeze tag, there was hardly any point
for the rest of us boys to run—we knew who she would be chasing.
He wore the latest Swatch for a timepiece, and as I recall he knew how
to efficiently "tight roll" his denim pant legs just above his sneakers.
And there was of course the gold chain glimmering in the V-shape
imposed onto his tanned chest by the polo shirts. (They were defi-
nitely made by Ralph Lauren and *not* the imitation brands.)

I did not stand a chance.

Strangely enough, he and I were friends. In the previous year the
teacher had sentenced him to move his seat from the back of the classroom in order to sit by the shy, squeamish kid who was too harmless
to pose any trouble. That was me, and due to his spatial relocation we
developed a bit of a friendship. But now, a year later, he had effort-
lessly secured as his girlfriend the one dazzling gem who had become
the object of all my romantic hopes.

One night he called me and confessed to cheating on her. (I was
never sure what this entailed during the middle school years, but it
always sounded so sinister.) The next day, his betrayal was the big
scandal, and my chance had come to rise to the surface as an alternative suitor. All day long I stood by the distressed damsel as a valiant
guardian against all male evils, repeatedly hinting to her that should

she choose to "go with" *me*, she would never have to face the pain of mistreatment again. By lunchtime it seemed as though the entire sixth grade class was involved in this thrilling imbroglio.

Then at the end of the day, through the clang and bang of the hallway lockers, she broke the news to me with laughter that it was all staged—our classmates knew about my (supposedly secret) crush, and they just wanted to see how I would react to the fictional scenario. The spectacle I had provided went beyond their grandest expectations.

For years to come I was a romantic cynic.

There are much darker adolescent tales out there than my unpleasant little introduction to teenage romance. The story is provided to make the point that cynicism often arises from painful disillusionment—when the rug gets violently jerked out from under us, when the wool long pulled over our eyes is yanked off. The moment of the defining injury is often abrupt, having the effect of an explosive collision that tosses us into some pit. When we open our eyes after the impact, we find ourselves in a dark place staring up into a light we once enjoyed—and to which we feel we can never return.

Sometimes the painful disillusionment is not abrupt but subtle, gradually developing within us over time like the imperceptible infiltration of a slow-working virus. Then one day it occurs to us that we have become all too familiar with a darkness we never knew took us over, and we barely recognize the light.

Then again, was it really "light" from which we fell? Disillusionment is the dispersal of illusions. What we violently collide with before the sharp plummet into cynicism's pit is usually a disturbing reality. If the downward movement is more gradual, then our cynicism has resulted from accepting a series of disquieting truths over a period of months or years. Cynicism arises from an embrace of reality. But since illumination often hurts, it can become an *embittered* embrace of reality.

I eventually recovered from my bout with romantic disillusionment. (And I should point out the fact that the young teenage girl in the previous scene is now serving Christ nobly on the mission field.) There is a form of disillusionment that is much more potentially devastating than that of crushed romance, though. What if we are disillusioned by the *church*—that one safe harbor of community on which Christians are told to rely when all else comes crashing down? What if we become cynical toward the *faith* that is supposed to sustain us through all life's trials? Even worse, what if the object of our disillusionment is not the thirteen-year-old dream girl we adore, the spouse we treasure, or the church that (supposedly) nurtures us, *but the God we worship?*

(CHRISTIAN) CYNICISM: A SPIRITUAL SICKNESS?

Cynicism is rampant in secular culture. It also flourishes among Christians, and this book is concerned with the "Christian" version of cynicism. Though there is indeed a great deal of disenchantment with God these days, "Christian" cynicism seems most often directed toward the church. As an untidy conglomeration of imperfect people from all walks of life, the margin for human error in the church is quite high, isn't it? We are a dysfunctional family of sinful siblings, repeatedly failing and injuring one another. Christians must constantly nurse in-house wounds. Thus the descent, whether immediate or gradual, into cynicism.

So many believers have now slid into those dark pits that cynicism is becoming vogue in many Christian circles as a self-identifying trademark of a new spirituality—the edgy spirituality of the jaded. Since cynicism is emerging as a hip new way to be "spiritual," religious disenchantment is often hailed as a spiritual virtue.

How do we identify cynical Christians? They would never be caught in public wearing the ridiculous T-shirt they got at that legalistic dating conference from earlier days in the youth group. Christian cynics would be humiliated if anyone found the old "What Would Jesus Do?" bracelet buried in their desk drawer. They would listen to the Christian pop music radio station only for laughs. They would try to avoid displaying too much emotion during a worship service or answering correctly too many questions at the Bible study, lest they

Ha!

suffer from the dreaded accusation of being "hyperspiritual."

On a graver note, Christian cynics sometimes delight in watching fellow believers tread on life's land mines, and their flaunted skepticism can even become the means by which the faithful forsake their faith.

For obvious reasons the anti-institutional attitude of cynicism does not comport well with the established church. Cynical Christians are therefore situated on the fringes of Christian fellowship. Their position on the margins allows them to be close enough to the church to (often amusingly) criticize its mistakes while maintaining a degree of allegiance to Jesus (whose harangues against the established religious leadership of his day become favorite Scripture passages). Cynics praise themselves for taking the red pill of "reality," and then they stick it to "the Man" by unplugging themselves from the "matrix" of the institutional church.[1]

But who does the Christian cynic "stick it to" if "the Man" is Jesus himself or the church he died for? *Woah* ?

Such questions expose cynicism as potentially misguided and dangerous. Cynics have been wounded, or at least frustrated, and their edgy spirituality is the spirituality of those whose spiritual wounds and frustrations have become infected, when their *brokenness* has soured into *bitterness*.

Cynicism is a sickness.

To be cynical is to be "contemptuously distrustful of human nature and motives."[2] Why is the temperament *contemptuous?* Because some defining experience usually provides the empirical evidence for becoming distrustful—and it hurts. Some of us, of course, have personalities more disposed to cynicism than others. But it is important to note that full-blown cynicism among Christians toward God or the church is often triggered by some revealing experience or series of events that hurts us and eventually impairs our spiritual health.

For the purposes of this book we could attempt to define cynicism as *an* embittered disposition of distrust born out of painful disillusionment. To be cynical is to be spiritually ill. But it is not terminal. Christian cynics, injured somehow in relation to their faith, need not go untreated. Wounds can heal. If preventative measures are taken, the painful disillusionment does not even have to lead to cynicism in the first place.

POP CHRISTIANITY AND THE GIFT OF DISILLUSIONMENT

Is all cynicism unhealthy, though? Could there be a form of cynicism that is actually beneficial, perhaps even *biblical?*

Cynicism has reached epidemic status within the church, but it is not our only illness. Many of these other ailments plaguing the church are the very means by which cynics become cynical. The term *pop Christianity* appears from time to time, usually to refer to the oversimplified theology and the trite sentimentality that is so rife throughout the Western church. This is a populist version of Christianity that is "purged of complexities, nuance, and darkness" and lacking "poetry and emotional breadth."[3] Many illnesses can be identified under the rubric of pop Christianity, to which cynicism has become a common response.

But fighting sickness with sickness will just promote mass contagion.

This book is written with the conviction that the church is in need of corrective voices, but that cynical voices will hurt more than help. Are there alternative responses to pop Christianity that can promote healing in the church? Can we be discerning Christians without becoming full-blown cynics? Is there a way to critique and challenge the church more out of love than out of disgust?

Yes.

As long as pop Christianity is nurtured in the church, then Christians will be inadvertent accomplices in spreading the spiritual sickness of cynicism in our pews (and even beyond into the wider culture). But if we could prevent the disenfranchised masses from plunging into cynicism and actively seek the rehabilitation of those already diagnosed as cynics, then we would secure an army of voices within our own ranks that can provide brilliant insights which, if tempered with love, could possibly lead to the reformation and renewal that the Western church so desperately needs.

This is because Christians who have been disillusioned are among the most discerning people in the church. Disillusionment is *illumination*. Those moments of painful discovery are revelatory experiences from which others could benefit. Dietrich Bonhoeffer actually hailed disillusionment with the church as a divine *gift*. The crushing of unrealistic dreams about God's people (as well as ourselves) is an act of God's grace:

> Just as surely as God desires to lead us to a knowledge of genuine Christian fellowship, so surely must we be overwhelmed by a great disillusionment with others, with Christians in general, and with ourselves. . . . Only that fellowship which faces such disillusionment, with all its unhappy and ugly aspects, begins to be what it should be in God's sight, begins to grasp in faith the promise that is given to it. The sooner this shock of disillusionment comes to an individual and to a community the better for both.[4]

This great theologian passionately calls us to disillusionment. But for the disillusionment to bear its fruit, we have to embrace it without collapsing into cynicism. When we experience hurtful illumination and resist turning cynical, we may realize that we have been entrusted with a tremendous gift that can be used for the edification of the church. If we can manage to find healing and regain our footing a bit after the rug has been ripped out from beneath us, then we may be used by God to free others from faulty ideas about our faith. Redeemed cynics have much to offer.

The apostle Paul's revelatory encounter with Christ (Acts 9) disabused him of terrible misconceptions, and the degree to which the church has benefited from that disillusioning experience on the Damascus road is incalculable. Before his disillusionment became salutary, however, he endured three days of blindness. From what we know about Paul's impressive pedigree in Pharisaical Judaism, it does not seem like much of a stretch to suggest that those three days were profoundly miserable for him as the extent of his misunderstandings about God and his faith were exposed. At the height of his religious zeal he made the shocking discovery that he was violently at odds with the God he thought he was serving. After Ananias's visit, however, he was strengthened and, it would seem, rehabilitated enough to evade debilitating modes of cynicism in his legendary ministry as the apostle to the Gentiles. His disillusionment was a gift, the benefits of which we are still reaping today.

Those prone to cynicism possess insights that the church, sick with populist misconceptions and ridiculous practices, desperately needs. Their voices will only be helpful, though, if, like Paul after his epiphany on the Damascus Road, their wounds can be restored to health. We are in dire need for redeemed cynics to dress their wounds that they may rise up and flourish in the truths revealed to them for the health of the church and for the glory of God.

RISING TO HOPEFUL REALISM WHILE BETWEEN THE EDENS
Our Bibles are book-ended with paradise: creation in Genesis 1–2, then new creation in Revelation 21–22 (cf. Isaiah 65–66). We live in between the reality of the original Eden and the restored Eden. Pop Christianity tends to deny the reality of ex-Eden existence, offering trite and formulaic slogans and clichés that idealize our experience of faith and rightly ring foul in cynical ears. The attitude of cynicism, in contrast, denies the reality that God has promised new creation, that it is just around the corner and that it is making appearances in the here and now through the work of Christ and his Spirit. We need to foster a biblical spirituality that embraces the grim reality of our ex-Eden life along with the joyful reality that God is making all things new. My wife calls this "hopeful realism." Promoting hopeful realism is the vision of this book.

The cynicism that arises from the moral failings of church leaders and the gossiping backbiting of parishioners could occupy an endless number of pages. This book, however, looks instead at the disappointing ways the church *thinks*. In part one, we will take an honest look at a number of clichés and trends of pop Christianity that fuel the angst and ire of Christian cynicism. We will identify a number of disappointing "isms" within the church that need reproof, while also considering how cynical responses to those "isms" are also in need of reproof. For instance, *anti-intellectualism* thrives in many Christian circles. This is unfortunate, but also unfortunate is *intellectual elitism*, a typical response from many a cynical Christian. My hope is that this section of the book will give voice to the frustrations of cynical readers, providing some degree of cathartic venting while at the same time providing convincing arguments that the standard cynical approaches are counterproductive.

Part two of the book presents biblical models for expressing corrective voices alternative to the approach of cynicism. Scripture vividly portrays the people of God as a community prone to wander and ever in need of renewal and reform. Scripture also offers guidance on the *proper means* of promoting that renewal and reform. Convinced that those prone to cynicism actually have much to offer the church, I provide alternative models of critique by contrasting the cynic with the biblical examples of the prophet, the sage and of those tragic poets behind the biblical lament literature. Since no voice is more pressing to hear than the voice of the One who loves the church enough to die for it, this section closes with a look at how Jesus himself addressed misconceptions and wrestled with his own disappointments with his followers—and also with his Father.

The book ends with a closer look at "hopeful realism," which the resurrection of our Lord makes possible for us to embrace instead of cynicism. We will study how Paul avoided cynicism (while serving dysfunctional local churches) because of his keen awareness that resurrection changes everything. We may live on the dark, eastern edge of Eden, but new creation awaits, and for the hopeful realists who have eyes to see and ears to hear, it keeps bursting into the present.

Before moving beyond introductory concerns into part one, however, I share an account of one of my own Damascus Road–type experiences of disillusionment. The romantic cynicism that ensued after my sixth grade heartbreak was mild compared to the spiritual cynicism I fell into after college. The defining moments of hurtful illumination came as a series of destructive blasts that left me spiritually disoriented. It took a few years before I reopened the wounds for therapeutic cleansing. Like Saul, I was on a journey motivated by fierce religious zeal. But it took me much longer than three days to recover my sight.

DISCUSSION QUESTIONS

1. Which of the following best describes you? (1) A cynic hoping to find biblical responses to that which frustrates you. (2) Someone trying to understand why cynics are cynical. (3) Someone trying to understand why you waver in and out of cynicism from time to time. Explain your choice.

2. What is something you are at least slightly cynical of? Why?

3. Do you believe cynicism can be labeled a "sickness" in need of a cure? Explain.

4. What damage have you seen cynicism do to yourself, to others or to the church?

5. Can you think of any biblical instances of cynicism?

checking into
the cynics' ward
with a fever of 360°

Oh, that I had wings like a dove!
  I would fly away and be at rest;
Yes, I would wander far away.

Psalm 55:6-7

He found himself wondering at times, especially in the autumn, about
the wild lands, and strange visions of mountains that he had never
seen came into his dreams. He began to say to himself: "Perhaps I
shall cross the river myself one day." To which the other half of his mind
always replied: "Not yet."

—J. R. R. Tolkien, *The Fellowship of the Ring*

I'm shakin' the dust of this crummy little town off my feet and I'm gonna
see the world.

—George Bailey, in *It's a Wonderful Life*

Being mortal had been such a problem for me.

For years I had harbored an underlying assumption that I had invisible wings, or that I could at least sprout a pair at will and fly away from the annoying limitations of mortal life.

When my undergraduate college career came to a close, it was with a strong sense of spiritual arrival. God had been revealing himself to me in dramatic fashion during those four years, enlivening my study of Scripture and thrilling me with a palpable sense of his presence. I had been reared in church, but the tender and yet terrifying God to whom I was being reintroduced in college was a God of truly biblical proportions, much grander and much less manageable than my former impressions allowed. I embraced a call to Christian ministry and longingly ached to serve him in grand fashion. This season of intense spiritual growth seemed preparatory for my entrance into the much-famed "real world," licensing me for spiritual grandeur.

Normal, everyday life seemed distastefully inferior for one so spiritually licensed.

I wanted to be plunged into God's mystical depths and thereby launched into the next level of spiritual maturity. For this to happen, I assumed I needed a qualifying experience of celestial scope. I was on the lookout for a spiritual gauntlet of sorts through which I would pass and then emerge winged and ready for divine flight. My impression of what this gauntlet should be had a geographical slant to it. Like Frodo Baggins holed up in Bag End, I found myself wistfully staring at maps and daydreaming of wild and distant lands.

In my spiritualized self-importance, I sensed God hinting that the time had come for me to take flight for those yonder hills. Along with Icarus, I managed to make arrangements for a set of wings. I did not paste feathers to my arms, but I *did* discover that the father of a friend of mine worked for a major airline. For a discounted price I ended up with standby tickets for a series of flights around the globe. Not exactly the wings I had in mind, but they would suffice in getting me off the ground.

The despised ground.

My itinerary included all 360 degrees of planet Earth. But the itinerary itself was not extreme enough for me. Four months before the departure date, I decided that God was telling me to stop working. I would nobly rely on his miraculous provision alone for my practical needs and for my upcoming travel expenses. I had stepped into my gauntlet.

Having sorely disappointed my own family with those plans to forgo a job search, I moved in with the family of a close friend who would be traveling with me. I lived off their extraordinary generosity while undergoing what became the most frustrating and confusing four months of my life up to that point. Gauntlets are by definition supposed to be hard—I knew that. But what plagued me most was the nagging sense that perhaps I was in the wrong gauntlet. *Was I doing the right thing?* Had God really called me to so sharply disappoint my family and to so enthusiastically rebel against the world's expectations for a young man just out of college? I was never confident of an answer. The words in my journal were carved into tear-stained pages by the brutal pressure of an angst-driven pen. Then one day, in an act of spiritual bravado, I decided that I would drink the cup to its last dregs, hopeful that once I embarked on the trip God would vindicate all my struggles and my unconventional decisions with the revelation that I had indeed taken the right path.

Financial provision did come at times, but that provision often lacked the glint and luster of "miracle" with which I had assumed it would be accompanied. Too often it arrived from the hands of those who patiently endured (and perhaps even pitied) my commitment to just stay in the basement of a kind family's home and pray all day over a stack of maps. Once a close friend brought up the sore subject of my finances—"So how much money do you have saved up for the trip?" I sheepishly told him about the small stack of pennies sitting on top of a desk back in the house where I was staying. One month before the scheduled departure, those sixty-six copper coins constituted the entirety of my personal savings.

Six months prior to this moment I had begun dating someone. She was beyond dreams. My delight in her was so deep that it painfully and joyfully pulsated in the marrow of my bones. Within two weeks of my initial flight date, she herself would be leaving on a plane to South America for almost a year of service on the mission field. My sick tendency to obsessively lose myself in fantastical daydreams of dread and doom left me with the notion that I would never see her again. She would be living in a remote village up in the Andes, and even though all the Ecuadorians I've met are sweet, nonviolent folks, I just knew she would be swept away in some night raid by marauding bandits.

Before dawn on January 2, 1997, the two of us rode to the Atlanta airport with my two travel companions and some supportive friends. I somehow mustered a presentable degree of composure by the boarding gate that morning and told my girlfriend that the next time I saw her I would ask her to marry me. With that, I turned away from her (it was the hardest move I have ever had to command my body to make) and without looking back (fashioned, of course, after Jesus' words about placing hands on plowshares), I walked onto a plane, bound for spiritual feats of global glory.

By that time I had pieced together just enough cash to make it 180 degrees around the world. It was stuffed into my pack when I boarded the plane. The problem was that there was another 180 degrees of the world for which I lacked any travel funds.

My bundle of cash lasted for six weeks.

For a handful of us, there are certain truths that cannot be learned except on the furthest side of the world. There is nothing like being stranded in Southeast Asia with a depleted purse for some keen introspection.

My traveling companions, some of my dearest friends from college, had departed, one back to his home in South Korea, one to begin seminary and the other to teach English in China. That left me in Singapore. I spent the nights sleeping on the floor of a small kindergarten classroom, an arrangement graciously provided through some contacts made after arriving in this Asian metropolis a few days earlier. I had to be out before the kids showed up for class, though, and since I had little money left for public transportation, I got a lot of walking in. I remember that one of my sandals was broken, so as I walked all over the city day after day, my pace was quite slow. This slowness of pace was only partially due to the broken strap on those sandals I had purchased for cheap in Bangkok; for the most part, it was due to the fact that I was as painfully disillusioned as I had ever been in my life.

The dust from the previous months had begun to settle during that lonely week in Singapore. I had been stretched and challenged more than ever before. The pain of disorientation was intensified by the fact that I was as far away as physically possible from my girlfriend. (Yes, I was a sentimental sap, my romantic cynicism having long since dissipated.) According to my handy little travel atlas, I was just above the equator in one hemisphere, and she was on the opposite side of the world just below the equator. (Yes, I took time to examine this distance regularly.) The last bit of money in my travel pouch had been initially reserved for the purchase of a modest engagement ring when I got to Ireland, my last stop before returning home. Singapore is a great city, but it is also an expensive city. If you are trying to save dollars and coins for an engagement ring, it's not an ideal location for getting stuck.

Unless, of course, God needs to stick you somewhere for instructional purposes.

With no vindication of the struggles from the previous months and with no spiritual exploits to boast in, clarity came to me as never before during that week. God was tearing a veil I never knew had been draped so thoroughly over me and from which I had enjoyed little freedom—until that awful and wonderful week in Singapore when I could hear and feel the unstitching of the fabric. The threads by which that dark pall had been woven were falsehoods that had shaped so much of what I had believed about God and spirituality, falsehoods that had largely motivated this odyssey to other side of the world.

The initial tears in the fabric began a couple of weeks earlier in Malaysia. From the sweltering heat of the urban coastline, we had traveled inland through mountainous forests to the village of Tanah Rata. Tucked into the folds of the Cameron Highlands, the milder climate and slower pace of this sleepy little town offered needed respite. Two of us were recovering from the uncomfortable and humbling effects of illness. We traced it to a parasite picked up from a pumpkin-pork dish we were served in the beautiful mountains of northern Thailand (nothing screams mortality like parasitic dysentery).

The sickness had left me dehydrated and weak, but one morning I feebly set off on a little hike. Though we had heard that tigers and other dangerous beasts roamed the forests, the parasite had sapped not only physical strength but also my aspirations for heroic adventures to write home about. So instead of charging into the wild I lingered around the fringes of the village.

I sauntered about until I found myself on a flat clearing notched out of the sloped edge of a mountainside. Beneath my feet was an old, crunched-up slab of concrete, probably the former site of a small house. Weeds were triumphantly asserting a dominance they had established long ago through the crumbling cracks and crevices. On the edge of that mountain this dilapidated concrete slab seemed like a defunct launching pad for those who had once aspired to flight. I prayed here for quite some time, wistfully eyeing bulging green mountains that I was too tired to conquer. Never before had my feet seemed more solidly attached to the ground.

The despised ground.

Never before had I so strongly felt the tyrannical hold of gravity on my ankles. There was no flying to be done. No magical cape whipped invisibly in the wind from my shoulders. I did not have wings.

Mortal.

So by the time I found myself aimlessly wandering the streets of Singapore, disillusioned with my perspectives on spirituality, pitifully missing my girlfriend and bedeviled by a bad sandal, I had been growing in the awareness that I had lived much of my life under the influence of grave delusions not only about God and my faith, but about myself.

I remember getting lost in a grocery store once as a little boy. The desperation to hear my mother's voice sharpened my sense of hearing during that frightening episode. That's similar to what happened to me in Southeast Asia. I was spiritually lost, and my frantic longing to hear from God was so acute that I eventually picked up his voice with rare clarity.

He showed me that I was on a journey he had already made.

I was on a trip to prove my devotion to him, to demonstrate my radical commitment and to get him to notice me and then to love me for my grandiose efforts. I was running a gauntlet I deemed prerequisite for entering into the next, more advanced stage of the spiritual life. My boarding of that first flight was the attempt to take a test and impressively pass it so God might be proud.

What I discovered in Singapore was that I was on a journey Jesus had already completed. He had already made the ultimate odyssey, and on my behalf. The points of departure had been cross and tomb. Through the work of Jesus, I was more than noticed by God—I was warmly adored. I was a holy creature beaming in the light of divine favor and delight. No proving gauntlet had been required of me. No sensational journey had been necessary.

I had to face the reality that in spite of what I deemed as impressive spiritual growth during college and in spite of that clear sense of calling to Christian ministry, I had a twisted understanding of both God and his gospel.

Three weeks and 180 degrees later I had made my way back home via planes, trains, buses, ferries, a pair of weary legs and much providential care. The duration of that journey in 1997 was only nine weeks, but there is no way to calculate the extent of its personal impact. In many ways I had encountered the blinding light of Christ on the road to Damascus. But my pride was so crushed by the degree to which I had misunderstood God and my faith that the revelations were difficult to appreciate. The massive gash ripped into my soul seemed too painful to process.

The wound still fresh and opened, I made a brief visit to the campus ministry so instrumental to my former spiritual growth. Many of my peers had respected my decision to launch off to the other side of the world for spiritual spoil. In my brokenness I wanted to admit to the misguided notions that had propelled me overseas. I wanted to communicate to my friends my newfound grasp of the gospel, that a great King had already performed the one adventure necessary to commend me before him forever.

What I found during my visit was the active promotion of many of those same misguided ideas. This was an incredibly powerful ministry that, generally speaking, was very healthy. I think I had made my visit during a brief season that did not last very long, and I believe the ministry is healthy and thriving today. But on the week of my particular visit, I remember a student speaker passionately proclaiming the very notions about God and spirituality that I had been rather painfully unlearning. To make matters worse, my friends were thanking me for the amazing "revival" they believed they were experiencing, attributing so much of its arrival to my previous four years of fervent intercession. *Was* this *what I had been praying for?* I did not know how to respond. So I walked away. As I did, my wounds of disillusionment grew deeper and began to sour.

Assuming I would heal just fine on my own, I soon embarked on that next chapter in life, which my journey had only postponed. This new season began with the joyful pledge of wedding vows to the girl beyond all dreams. And on the day after our honeymoon, I began seminary at Beeson Divinity School.

So I entered both marriage and seminary with deep wounds from painful disillusionment, and the brokenness was subtly metastasizing into bitterness. In reaction to my own former zeal, I became skeptical of anything that smacked of religious enthusiasm. Through my schooling I was gaining fascinating insights into theology, Scripture and spirituality that the wider church seemed largely blind to. Jaded by the skewed ideals of pop Christianity, many of which I had once embraced, I became increasingly cynical. Thankfully, Beeson is remarkably balanced in jointly emphasizing the heart along with the mind in theological education—otherwise my cynicism would have become even more severe. Even so, my earlier seminary years were marked by a suspicious annoyance toward the church I was being trained to serve.

As a sickness, cynicism is contagious. Before long, I noticed that the girl beyond dreams, who had graciously given me her hand in marriage, was beginning to display the symptoms. Even worse, I realized that her own passion for Christ and delight in his church were being inadvertently persecuted by my barrage of cynical remarks. It was time to check into the cynics' ward. It was time to heal, to lay open the stinking wounds before the surgeon and then submit to the rehab. It took a while.

Nothing heals like the awareness that God's love is large enough to embrace a church full of misguided failures, among whom I will ever be numbered. My discharge papers from the cynics' ward are now in hand.

DISCUSSION QUESTIONS

1. The author found himself alone and on the other side learning a tough lesson from God. What has been a similar situation in your life when you have had to learn something the hard way?

2. What has happened when your cynical comments or temperament has affected the people around you?

3. What temporary or lasting effects did someone's cynicism have on you?

part one

POP CHRISTIANITY

What Makes Us Cynical

As mentioned in chapter one, cynicism is a spiritual sickness that arises in response to other ailments endemic to the church. The chapters of part one look at a handful of these other illnesses that make themselves manifest through a disheartening menagerie of unrealistic clichés and platitudes repeated with alarming frequency in pop Christianity. Though this book's purpose is to discourage cynicism, it is not written to encourage a dismissive tolerance of these misconceptions. The way out of cynicism is not to pretend that populist expressions of Christianity are acceptable. But as a friend of mine has said, there can be a wrong way of being right. Let's be unafraid to call a spade a spade, but in such a way that our evaluations are ultimately constructive instead of destructive.

In no way are the trends addressed in this section exhaustive (we could add plenty more to the list!). Contemporary experience and the New Testament epistles together indicate that the church will be ever plagued with shallow or distorted ideas that others will respond to in both helpful and unhelpful ways. Hopefully the examinations found on the following pages will provide some sort of model for how we can provide careful critiques of the church without becoming part of just another bad trend ourselves.

3   # idealism

"Well, I . . . I want to believe . . .
but . . ."

   "But you don't want to be bamboozled.
You don't want to be led down the primrose path!
You don't want to be conned or duped. Have the wool
pulled over your eyes. Hoodwinked! You don't want to be
taken for a ride. Railroaded!"

—Exchange between the "boy" and the "hobo" from *The Polar Express*

It is impossible to understand our participation in salvation as a life of
untroubled serenity, a life apart from suffering, a life protected from
disruption, a charmed life, a life exempt from pain and humiliation
and rejection.

—Eugene Peterson, *Christ Plays in Ten Thousand Places*

The seven-year-old across the street realized that I still believed in a guy with a red suit and a sleigh who climbs down chimneys on Christmas Eve. Triumphantly, he took it upon himself to disabuse me of this fairytale, playing the role of enlightened escort as I passed into a cruel world in which Santa was no more than a cute legend sustained by parental sentimentality and holiday commercialism. This little neighbor was one year younger than me, and the delight he took in shredding the childhood beliefs of an older third-grader was quite obvious.

I did not believe him at first; but after doing the math, I had to admit to the plausibility of the case he presented. Some epiphanies come as a bright shining light. Others come as crashing waves, the floodgates of which we would prefer to keep closed.

I could not completely relinquish this childhood belief, however, until I had consulted those towering figures who had been nurturing the Santa cult in our household all my life—Mom and Dad. Not long before Christmas day, I was riding with my mother through the north Georgia countryside and reluctantly began a litany of life-altering questions:

"Mom, is the tooth fairy real?"

"No," she replied, but after a pause—her suspicions were raised and she seemed to have an idea about where this was going. She shifted in her seat and readied herself for the parental task at hand.

"The Easter Bunny?"

"No." This was after another pause.

I reflected on these negations for a moment, distastefully drawing the bitter cup of reality closer to my lips before posing the next question: "Then Santa—he isn't real either, is he?"

"No." My poor mother was now mourning all those years of fun surprises terminated prematurely by an overly zealous informant from the second grade.

She did not foresee my final question, and I did not immediately ask it. I had to steel myself for the answer, making certain that I really would rather know the truth than to live in the fantastical world of a child.

"Mom, I've just got to know—is *Jesus* real?"

Is Jesus real? A lot of people are asking this question, but there is often a long line of letdowns that stand in the way of hearing an affirmative answer. My dear mother broke out in tears and told me "Yes, yes, Jesus is real," but she knew that she could only affirm this from a shifty platform. After all, she had just brought solemn closure to all the other fantastical elements in my childhood that required belief. The world in which benevolent fairies gently placed cash under my pillow, in which a fluffy bunny brought eggs full of candy and those sticky marshmallow chicks, in which a jolly old soul magically traversed the globe leaving shiny, plastic treasures beneath aromatic evergreens— that utopian world was lost to me. The exodus from early childhood ideals comes with lots of tough questions: *Why do I have to get allergy shots every week? Why did we have to bury our dog? What is divorce? Granddaddy has cancer? What is that, Dad? Why is Mom sad?*

Is Jesus real?

FROM IDEALISM TO CYNICISM
(AND FROM MODERNITY TO POSTMODERNITY)

The most fertile soil for cynicism is its opposite pole of idealism. Though we tend to stereotype the modern-day cynic as abrasive and caustic, that rough-edged persona has usually emerged from a previous stage of earnest optimism.[1] Someone's susceptibility to cynicism is therefore related to the extent of their credulous idealism. The metamorphosis from idealist to cynic can actually happen overnight.

"Yes, yes, Jesus is real." My mother was urging me as a disillusioned eight-year-old to maintain belief *in Christ* while I relinquished other beliefs. Her attempts seemed not only illogical but also suspicious. How should I blindly believe in Jesus when my blind belief in the tooth fairy, the Easter Bunny and Santa had been exposed as unfounded? Why would my mom urge me to selectively believe in Jesus and yet excuse me from believing in the others? Was she trying to hide something? (My poor mom!)

When a dearly held expectation is proven no more than an idealistic pipe dream, we begin to doubt everything else that requires a degree of hopefulness and faith. My mother had to rush to perform damage control, to help me emerge from the ashes of crushed beliefs while salvaging my belief in Christ.

Ministers are regularly involved in this type of damage control, because much of what Christians believe is simply fantastical. Much is certainly true, of course, but we have developed our views on life and our theology through rather weak filters and failed to use Scripture as our primary foundation. Due to a variety of cultural and socioeconomic factors, many Western Christians have their hopes anchored in optimistic ideals that could only come from a God who wields a magic wand and brings a kingdom that strangely resembles the Magic Kingdom! This idealistic spirituality embraces the legitimate Christian realities of triumph, strength, deliverance, joy and happiness without also embracing the equally (and often more immediate) Christian realities of suffering, pain, struggle and weakness. By embracing this triumphalistic understanding of Christianity, we are (as mentioned earlier) unwittingly populating our pews and our world with jaded cynics, *because idealism is not tenable.* Our unrealistic expectations of what it means to live as people of faith in a fractured, dystopian, ex-Eden world is providing wind for the sails of many whose faith is on the edge of being shipwrecked.

Perhaps surprisingly, the most idealistic people in the Western world simultaneously share the same social environment as some of the most cynical people in the Western world—the university campus. Youthfulness is conducive to the formation of grand ideals. This is especially true when that youthfulness is accompanied with the privileged status enjoyed (whether realized or not) by the Western college student. They will energetically work with the homeless, organize night vigils, give all their (parents') money away and champion civil rights, all for the noble cause of making the world a better place. The passion accompanying this idealism is such that the college campus is one of the most exhilarating settings in the world.

It is also one of the most insulated settings in the world. Idealism can thrive when you don't have to make mortgage payments, worry with Medicaid paperwork or determine what's wrong with the screaming baby you just brought home from the hospital. The microcosmic nature of the campus setting postpones certain inevitable frustrations, allowing idealism to flourish.

Except when the insular layer is sometimes cracked open. Many college students endure tremendous financial stress and some *do* come home from hospitals with new babies in their arms. The bright shining future in the business world can become darkened when the Accounting 101 test is returned with a blood-red "F" at the top of the page (written from experience!). The party that seemed so innocently vivacious can produce lifelong regrets. Walls demarcate the property boundaries of many school campuses, but they do not provide an impenetrable shield against the brutal harshness of this fallen world. The most violent killing spree in U.S. history took place just a few years ago, and it was on a university campus.

Our grand ideals often fail to withstand the onslaughts of life's vicissitudes from which not even privileged college students are immune. In search of an alternative way to interpret life, the disillusioned will often emerge from the broken shards of busted-up idealism to don the protective armor of cynicism.

The terms *postmodernism* and *postmodernity* refer to a complicated worldview in response to the ideals that modernism/modernity promised yet failed to deliver.[2] These promises stem from the Enlightenment-era understanding of history as a linear progression toward something greater than the past, toward a brighter, better future capably engineered by humankind. Sophisticated Western society is built on this guiding hope that everything is in a constant state of progression and improvement, if sufficient control is exerted over all the moving variables. The most basic elements of capitalism are driven by this modern expectation—the entire idea of a stock market only works if the promise of future improvement is embraced and believed in. Our personal financing is based on this ideal that life is ever improving. We buy a house with the expectation that we will be able to make the mortgage payments for the next several years, and should we choose to resell, we assume that appreciation will bring us a rewarding payoff. Our political system is driven by these idealistic assumptions—what politician runs without the rhetoric of making things better, ending the war, decreasing the unemployment numbers, widening the job market or cleaning up the environment? This is the language of a possible and emerging utopia. We are progressing toward perfection, and soon we will arrive. Just a few more stories to add onto Babel's tower.[3]

This idealistic hopefulness, however, is proven time and time again as false (thus *post*modernity).[4] Pick up the daily paper or turn on the news program, anytime, anywhere: corporate scandals, wild raids by obscure militia groups, flagrant immorality, broken ceasefires, human trafficking, rigged athletic games, epidemic outbreaks and natural disasters. The impressive technological advances since the Industrial Revolution seem quite incapable of curbing evil in our world. Postmodernity should actually be welcomed to the extent that it decries the humanistic idealism of modernity to be a sham.[5] It is becoming increasingly more difficult for our society to sustain idealism since so many of us have ended up flat on our backs after having the carpet of our ideals jerked out from beneath our feet.

But as with many *r*eactions, postmodernism can be an *over*reaction. When modernity's promises fall so short, the result is often a freefall into a cynical abyss. When it is revealed that "the dominant myth by which the whole modern age has lived—the idea of historical progress—has not only failed us but turned against us," then where will we turn?[6] Having so few other options, many of us will choose the skepticism and distrust of postmodern cynicism.

And, as we have seen, the perfect candidate for this disenchantment is the *idealist*.

POP CHRISTIANITY AND IDEALISM IN THE CHURCH: DISASSEMBLY REQUIRED

Along with nurturing Santa belief (or consoling Santa disbelief), parents of young children have a lot of other work to do around Christmas time. After the shopping and wrapping, there is much "Assembly Required."

In the life of the church, though, we are in need of some disassembly. We need to begin dismantling our unbiblical ideas about ourselves, our world and our Lord.

We believe strongly that God has made humankind as the crowning joy of his creative artistry. We affirm that his creation teems and shimmers with beauty that declares his praise. And we uphold that he is a God who rescues, redeems and restores. But we have allowed these sound beliefs to be twisted and tweaked by unsound claims from humanism and modernity. We tend to idealize humanity and the world we live in, which creates twisted expectations that our view of God must conform to. These unrealistic ideas show up in our feel-good sermons, our trivializations of suffering and in the constant flow of our peppy, motivational lingo.

So, disassembly is required in our view of humanity (anthropology), in our view of the world (cosmology) and in our view of God (theology). Disentangling our culture's ideas from our Bible's affirmations is tedious work, but let's give it a go.

1. Idealized anthropology: "You can do anything you put your mind to!" As a father of four young children, I have become more convinced than ever of the Christian doctrine that humans are made in the image of God. My wife and I are astounded daily by a magnitude of beauty in our kids' faces, comments and actions, which are sourced in divine, supernatural craftsmanship.

We are also more convinced than ever of the Christian doctrine of original sin! One moment our children are holding hands and lovingly serving one another, and then within a flash they are bickering and yelling at one other. Made in God's image, *yes*. Sinful and corrupt, *yes*.

Anthropology asks the question, who am I? Who are we as human beings? We find the anthropology question in Psalm 8:4: "*what is man* that you are mindful of him, / and the son of man that you care for him?*" (emphasis added). The answer supplied by the psalmist asking the question affirms the doctrine that we are made in God's image, and thereby entrusted with the stewardship of creation (cf. Gen 1:26-31):

> You have made him a little lower than the heavenly beings
> and crowned him with glory and honor.

You have given him dominion over the works of your hands;
    you have put all things under his feet,
all sheep and oxen,
    and also the beasts of the field,
the birds of the air, and the fish of the sea,
    whatever passes along the paths of the seas. (Psalm 8:5-8)

There are many people out there who need to hear that we are wondrous beings created for God's pleasure and fashioned after him in such a way that we can relate to him and participate in his work in the world.

This positive anthropology that we are made in the *imago Dei* (Latin for "image of God"), however, does not license us to be *too* impressed with ourselves. Celebrating the God-given beauty of humankind is always just a spit away from distorting into the humanistic teaching of modernity that we are God-independent and sufficient in and of ourselves to achieve and succeed. Still ringing in the ears of those of us who grew up in middle- and upper-class households is that mantra from our childhood: "You can do anything you put your mind to."

Really?

Along with Psalm 8, the anthropology question is also asked in James 4:13-14:

Come now, you who say, "Today or tomorrow we will go into such and such a town and spend a year there and trade and make a profit"—yet you do not know what tomorrow will bring. *What is your life?* For you are a mist that appears for a little time and then vanishes. (Emphasis added)

Who am I? What is my life? Whereas modernity's (very American) answer to the anthropology question is "You can do anything you put your mind to," James says rather, "You are a mist."

A mist. A vapor. A wisp of air barely perceptible and then gone.[7] No matter if we are young or old, our disappearance is currently underway.

Though we humans are marvelous creatures made in the divine image, we cannot adopt an *anthropology* that is not subordinated to our *theology*. In other words, we must always view ourselves in relation to the One in whose image we are made. The anthropology of Psalm 8 is bracketed in the opening and closing verses with the superior concern of theology: "O LORD, our Lord, / how majestic is your name in all the earth!" (Psalm 8:1, 9). And James adds that instead of presumptuously embarking on our self-made plans, we should seek that our agenda is aligned with the divine agenda: "Instead you ought to say, 'If the Lord wills, we will live and do this or that'" (James 4:15). We may be made in God's image, but we are not gods ourselves. Scripture repeatedly reminds us of our smallness and our transience:

> Surely the nations are like a drop in a bucket;
> > they are regarded as dust on the scales;
> he weighs the islands as though they were fine dust. . . .
>
> Before him all the nations are as nothing;
> > they are regarded by him as worthless
> and less than nothing. (Isaiah 40:15, 17 NIV)

Biblical anthropology stands in dissonant contrast with the American anthropology inculcated into our minds since childhood that seems to disregard human limitations.

This idealizing of ourselves tends to deny not only our natural limitations but our moral sinfulness. Though we are made in God's image, that image has been marred and damaged by sin. Ignoring the nightmarish reality of original sin sets us up for grave disappointment in ourselves and in others.[8]

A few years ago I was standing on a railway track, now out of service, wondering if I should explode in tears or in shouts of anger. I had never seen a track like this one. It was unique because of its abrupt dead-end at a stand of trees. The track just stopped. Flanking its terminus were the remains of two large furnaces once used to incinerate fathers, mothers, daughters, sons and grandparents into ash. I was in the Auschwitz complex, standing on the railway line that came to such a blunt end at the Birkenau camp.

The Holocaust is one of the many atrocities of the twentieth century that convincingly evidences the Christian doctrine that the human heart is collectively disfigured by sin. In spite of the undeniable evidence, though, there are many Christian leaders who seem to promote an idealized anthropology, inspiring us to grab life by the horns like good Americans and live our lives to the fullest, in denial of the fact that deep in our hearts is the potential for committing Holocaust-style atrocities. Trinkets in Christian bookshops are emblazoned with charming snippets that drip thick with this humanistic idealism. Many of our sermons are little more than secular motivational speeches clothed with Christian rhetoric and proof-texted with obscure Bible verses. The church is consuming books on how to succeed and how to lead, eagerly allowing secular humanism to shape and nurture an arrogant anthropology that says "today or tomorrow" (James 4:13) I will achieve, make a lot of money and define my own destiny.

When I was in high school, kids started wearing T-shirts with the emblem of a large, bright smiley face. The wide, warm grin in that soft, soothing yellow conveyed the message "Be happy—everything is going to be okay."

And then other T-shirts began appearing with the exact same smiley face image except for one additional graphic: a bloodied bullet hole in the forehead! This image was a response to the unrealistic idealism of a permanent smile aglow in happy yellow. The "Life is Good" franchise seems to be quite successful nowadays, but those products are only marketable to a certain segment of our society—you don't see the poor with "Life is Good" bumper stickers on their cars—if they have cars, that is. Cynicism's alternative slogans of "Life Sucks" and "S___ Happens" are admittedly a bit harsh, but the cynicism might not be so harsh were the distorted idealism to which it responds not so excessively flowery.

2. Idealized cosmology: Living the "victorious Christian life."
Cosmology refers to our view of the world. One person in my life who does not have an idealistic view of the world is my grandmother. The Great Depression that intensified her rural poverty, the Second World

War that temporarily took away her newly married husband, the day-to-day struggle of farm life, the persistent shadow of death that prematurely took away siblings and friends have all prevented her from viewing life through rose-colored glasses.

One day I gave her a call and told her I was about to embark on the four-hour journey to her house: "Hey Grandmother—it's me, Andy!"

"Hey, hon."

"I'm about to come and visit you, but it's a long drive so don't be expecting me until much later tonight."

"Well, don't get in a wreck."

"Don't worry, I'll be careful."

"Well, don't fall asleep and run off the road."

"Don't worry. If I get sleepy I'll pull off at a gas station."

"Well, don't get shot."

How was I to respond to her warnings? On the one hand the pessimism seemed exaggerated, but on the other there certainly are terrible wrecks every day, many people do run off the road, and each time we watch the local news we are reminded that gas station shootings certainly do take place. (Though the chances that all three would happen to me during my four-hour drive may have been on the low side!)

I could have assured my grandmother that everything would be fine. After all, I'm a Christian, and "he who is in [us] is greater than he who is in the world," right (1 John 4:4)?

Just as there is tension in biblical anthropology (we are made in God's image, yet that image is marred by sin), there is also tension in biblical cosmology—God created the world good, but it, too, is marred by sin. While hiking on a mountain with a friend, I told him how I always strive to hear the sound of creation declaring God's praise when I am outdoors. "I do the same," he said, "but I also strive to hear the sound of creation *groaning*." It was a good reminder of the cosmological teaching we find from Paul that all creation is "subjected to futility," in "bondage to decay" and "groaning" with anticipation for the completion of God's redeeming work (see Romans 8:20-22). After the Fall in Genesis 3, God told Adam that the "ground" (seman-

tically connected to "Adam" in the Hebrew) is cursed because of him
(v. 17). Its regular produce would be "thorns and thistles" (v. 18). So
we now live in a plague world that is "beset by a kind of spiritual en-
tropy."[9] HIV, AIDS, murder, war, child abuse, extortion, fist fights,
alcoholism, drug addiction and the like. What else could be expected
from a world that has staged a cosmic mutiny, detaching itself in bla-
tant arrogance from its benign Creator?

The groaning of creation is so raucous and unsettling that most of
us would prefer to clasp our hands over our ears or crank up the vol-
ume on our iPod just a few more clicks. And those of us who can afford an iPod to crank up probably live in environments that have been
carefully designed to squelch out the noise of creation's groaning.
Manicured lawns and carefully drafted zoning laws help us to become
more easily convinced that all is well. Sometimes, the only visual evidence we have of the fallenness of our world is the roadkill we pass on
the way to the mall.

As cultural inheritors of a hopeful, modern cosmology that assures
that everything is improving and progressing, Western Christians are
tempted to assume that our faith somehow immunizes us from the
effects of a creation that the Bible portrays as *sick*. When the raw ter-
ror of the world roars through disaster and disease, Christians sometimes respond only with paralysis and speechlessness. We are inar-
ticulate in the face of despair because idealistic spirituality leaves little
room for pain, the pain that must inevitably accompany life in a world
that has arrogantly denied its Maker.

When we do attempt to say something in the face of creation's terrible groaning, our words tend to trivialize tragedy. We offer insub-
stantial platitudes that must sound so banal and empty in the ears of
the suffering. Funeral homes are echoing with well-meaning but often
insipid phrases like "this happened for a reason," "it will all turn out
for the best" or "tomorrow is a new day." We then encourage one another to buck up and embrace what sometimes gets referred to as "the
victorious Christian life."

There is nothing wrong with affirming that a Christian can live victoriously in a fallen world—unless the understanding of *victory* is more secular than it is biblical. Unfortunately, this "victorious Christian life" is often presented as a Christianized version of the American dream. The victory granted us in the world, however, is not *escape from* pain and suffering, but *strength to endure* pain and suffering. The victorious Christian is not someone who has made a lot of money, found a "hot" spouse, and evaded disease and injury. The victorious Christian is one who is clinging so tightly to Christ as the highest treasure that he or she can be "content" in "whatever situation" (Philippians 4:11). We love to quote "I can do all things through him who strengthens me" (Philippians 4:13), but we easily forget that those words came from someone in a prison cell, and God had strengthened him to learn "the secret of facing plenty *and hunger*, abundance *and need*" (Philippians 4:12, emphasis added).

The beauty of the world is striking in its mountainscapes, glacial gorges and expansive plains. Also striking is the horrific degree to which our world groans and pulsates with natural disasters, systemic oppression and hopeless shantytowns. Idealistic views of ourselves and our world may flourish temporarily in healthier and wealthier demographic slices. But if our gospel cannot speak to Auschwitz, if it cannot speak to marauded villages in the eastern Congo, if it cannot speak in the ears of abducted children, if it cannot make sense to mothers digging for children in earthquake rubble, then it ought not sound forth from polished pulpits in carpeted suburban sanctuaries. Sadly, the kind of message that is embraced so readily in poorer, oppressed places in the world are exported versions of the Western health and wealth and prosperity gospel, which will always prove to be no more than idealistic pipe dreams in the end.

3. Idealized theology: "God will never give you more than you can handle." Our view of God should shape our view of ourselves and our world. Unfortunately, we often opt for the other way around. Once we embrace an idealized anthropology that assumes good things happen to good people who work hard to succeed, and once we adopt an idealized cosmology that leaves little room for pain and suffering, then we begin making assumptions about the God who has supposedly secured all these cheery arrangements. We end up with an idealized God, a God who "never gives us more than we can handle." We begin making broad generalizations premised on our idealized theology, like "my God would never allow that." We begin making promises on behalf of this idealized God like "your daughter will be healed of her cancer." If idealistic anthropology has little room for the addict who never recovers and if idealistic cosmology has little room for a world full of tsunamis and holocausts, then idealized theology leaves little room for the tough reality of divine silence and unanswered prayers.

I was once gathered with a handful of friends from church when someone shared how he miraculously escaped a collision with an oncoming vehicle. He was riding his bike through an intersection and never saw the car speeding right toward him. After a few abrupt maneuvers, the intersection was traversed by all parties with no injuries. We rejoiced with our friend, praising God that he had been rescued from disaster.

Then it occurred to me that sitting among us was another dear friend who has been permanently injured because she *had not* escaped a collision. A car violently hit her while she was walking across a street. I wondered how she felt about the praise given to God for deliverance when a few years earlier she had not been delivered herself.

Our theology must be capacious enough for a God who is sovereign over episodes of both rescue and defeat. "The LORD gave, and the LORD has taken away; blessed be the name of the LORD" (Job 1:21). God himself makes this striking declaration in Isaiah 45:7:

> I form light and create darkness,
> I make well-being and create calamity,
> I am the LORD, who does all these things.
> (See also Deuteronomy 32:39.)

Hannah acknowledged in her prayer, "The LORD kills and brings to life; / he brings down to Sheol and raises up" (1 Samuel 2:6). Are we willing to worship a God who refuses conformity to our idealism?

OF WHOM THE WORLD WAS NOT WORTHY

My wife and I became very close to a college student named Pamela whose joyous, enormous faith inspired and challenged us. After a life of perfect health, she ended up in a hospital bed with the surprising diagnosis of Crohn's disease. She temporarily withdrew from school to regain her strength as best as possible. She had to begin adjusting to a new diet and an altered lifestyle, one besieged by the effects of an incurable illness.

Within the year, she triumphantly returned to school, inspiring us all with her faith in Christ's power to strengthen her and enable her to live victoriously in spite of her condition. But Pamela began to discover the fine line that so many plagued with chronic sickness must pay such tedious attention to—the line between accepting her condition while discerning Christ in the midst of it, or denying her condition while seeking Christ as the Physician who will always heal.

Claiming insight into the divine scheme of things, some people had begun intimating that God was going to cure her soon. Victory and triumph awaited if she maintained faith.

But Pamela began to be skeptical about such promises. Was it because she was weak in faith? Some would have said so. But she detected something that seemed spurious in the talk of her impending miraculous cure. She longed for it (we all did), but she sensed that God was actually calling her to embrace the sickness, to live victoriously through it, not to live victoriously solely by the hope of escaping it. So the focus of our prayers changed a bit. Along with praying for miraculous *curing*, we also began to pray for miraculous *endurance*.

The latter prayer was answered. *Only* the latter prayer.

As she endured, she became increasingly adjusted to her circumstances, and there were long seasons when she felt fairly normal in spite of her diagnosis. She began memorizing Paul's letter to the Philippians with my wife, and could easily cite that verse mentioned earlier: "I can do all things through him who strengthens me" (Philippians 4:13).

But she also knew well Philippians 1:21—"For me to live is Christ, and to die is gain."

After a year and a half of enduring her sickness faithfully, Pamela suddenly ended up in another hospital bed with a new diagnosis—lymphoma. A few weeks later we heard the news. She is with us no longer.

At her graveside service, I read from Hebrews 11. This is one of the most triumphant passages in the New Testament, called the "faith chapter" because it grandly recalls Old Testament heroes who

> through faith conquered kingdoms, enforced justice, obtained promises, stopped the mouths of lions, quenched the power of fire, escaped the edge of the sword, were made strong out of weakness, became mighty in war, put foreign armies to flight. Women received back their dead by resurrection. (Hebrews 11:33-35)

This is the kind of triumph and victory we are hoping for, the kind of religious experience we want to make our own. This is marketable faith, the kind that sells.

But there beneath the water oaks next to Pamela's freshly dug grave, I continued reading:

> some were tortured, refusing to accept release, so that they might rise again to a better life. Others suffered mocking and flogging, and even chains and imprisonment. They were stoned, they were sawn in two, they were killed with the sword. They went about in skins of sheep and goats, destitute, afflicted, mistreated—of whom the world was not worthy—wandering about in deserts and mountains, and in dens and caves of the earth. (Hebrews 11:35-38)

We cannot read the triumph and joy of Hebrews 11:33-35a without the torture and hurt of 11:35b-38. Our God gives—and takes away. Some receive back their dead by resurrection, but others mourn beneath water oaks by freshly dug graves.

Is Jesus real?

The answer is no if we are talking about a Christ who "will never give us more than we can handle." This phrase is offered as consolation with the regularity of a favored Bible verse. Though the intentions are commendable, the theology is a bit off. I think the idea comes from 1 Corinthians 10:13—"No temptation has overtaken you that is not common to man. God is faithful, and he will not let you be tempted beyond your ability, but with the temptation he will also provide the way of escape, that you may be able to endure it."

Behind the English *temptation* and *be tempted* in this verse are the Greek words *peirasmos* and *peirazō*. A *peirasmos* can refer to a trial. If this were the case in 1 Corinthians 10:13, then "God will never give you more than you can handle" would be an appropriate paraphrase. It is clear from the context, however, that the noun and verbal form of the word refers to "temptation" and "being tempted"— the following verse 14 reads, "Therefore, . . . flee from idolatry." Paul is urging the Corinthian believers to resist the temptation to participate in the idolatrous practices of their surrounding culture, drawing from Israel's exodus wanderings as examples. So what God will never give us more than we can handle is *the temptation to sin*, specifically, in 1 Corinthians 10:13, the temptation to commit idolatry. The text is about escaping sin's difficult temptations, not about escaping the world's difficult circumstances. Paul actually found that God will sometimes give us *way* more than we can handle for the purpose of disassembling our self-reliance and establishing reliance on God alone: "For we were so utterly burdened *beyond our strength* that we despaired of life itself. . . . But that was to make us rely not on ourselves but on God who raises the dead" (2 Corinthians 1:8-9, emphasis added).

Suggesting that "God will never give us more than we can handle" promotes an idealized view of God. But in construing Paul's words on avoiding idolatry in 1 Corinthians 10:13 as idealized theology we become guilty of idolatry ourselves. To idealize God is to idolize a false god. *Idealized theology is idolatry.*

Is Jesus real? This depends—are we talking about an idealized Jesus who gives us fancy homes if only we ask in faith, or the Jesus of Scripture who told a would-be disciple "foxes have holes, and birds of the air have nests, but the Son of Man has nowhere to lay his

head" (Luke 9:58)? Yes, Jesus is real, and sometimes he cures people. But sometimes he doesn't. He grants many of our requests in
prayer. But not all of them. The most heartfelt prayer ever lifted in
history was his own, and it was unanswered—"Father, if you are
willing, remove this cup from Me" (Luke 22:42). And the next day
he became "Christ crucified" (1 Corinthians 1:23), not *Christ idealized*. Can we worship this Lord who gives and takes away, who was
himself taken in the night and then given no aid on Golgotha?
Blessed be the name of *this* Lord?

Elie Wiesel's *Night* is a brutalizing narrative that emerged from his
faith-destroying years in Nazi concentration camps.[10] In the foreword
of a 1960 edition, François Mauriac writes about his response to
Wiesel's recollection of a scene when a child was heartlessly hanged
before the entire prisoner population of the camp at Buna. Mauriac's
perspective is distinctly Christian, and he is able to see what Wiesel
could not see in that scene. But his response is not to paint a prettier
picture, to downplay the pain of the memory or to speak of an idealistic god who can help Wiesel pull himself up by the bootstraps. His
response is to consider "Christ crucified":

> And I, who believe that God is love, what answer could I give
> my young questioner, whose dark eyes still held the reflection of
> that angelic sadness which had appeared one day upon the face
> of the hanged child? Did I speak of that other Israeli, his brother,
> who may have resembled him—the Crucified, whose cross has
> conquered the world? Did I affirm that the stumbling block to
> his faith was the cornerstone of mine, and that the conformity
> between the Cross and the suffering of men was in my eyes the
> key to that impenetrable mystery whereon the faith of his child-
> hood had perished?[11]

The "impenetrable mystery" of our faith is that Christ has "con-
quered the world" through a cross. The victory of the "victorious
Christian life" has been secured not by escaping pain but by embracing pain's deepest depths.

RESETTING OUR ESCHATOLOGICAL CLOCKS

We've looked at how modernity has influenced Christian thinking on anthropology, cosmology and theology. We close the chapter looking at how idealists and cynics alike struggle with the eschatological question *when?*

Eschatology refers to "the end of the world as we know it."[12] Modernity has preached a message of hope and gradual improvement, but that hope has been lodged in human ingenuity. Biblical eschatology places no confidence in mortal endeavors. All hope is placed on that definitive moment when God, and God alone, will storm into our midst to make right all that sin has made wrong. All perversions, distortions, tragedies and maladies will meet their end when the divine reign is universalized and extended into every corner of the cosmos. A theological term for this event is the *parousia*—it refers to Christ's glorious and certain return. Revelation describes the result of this return as a re-created paradise mirroring that of Eden's garden.

One of the reasons the idealized spirituality we are addressing in this chapter is wrong is because it is eschatologically premature. The New Testament teaches that the *complete* actualization of God's will being done "on earth as it is in heaven" (Matthew 6:10) awaits the future. Idealism jump-starts the mysterious, divine chronology by answering the eschatological question *when* with *now*. We already have what is needed for utopia in our own brains and brawn—we just need to dig deep, tap into it, then release it. This overrealized eschatology fails to acknowledge that we are post-Eden and still pre-parousia.

Cynicism, however, seems to answer the eschatological *when* with *never*. Idealistic spirituality may offer eschatologically premature promises that are eventually broken. But these broken promises should not discredit the Bible's teaching on an approaching idealistic age in which

the wolf shall dwell with the lamb,
    and the leopard shall lie down with the young goat,
and the calf and the lion and the fattened calf together;

and a little child shall lead them.
(Isaiah 11:6; see also Isaiah 65:25)

The promises concerning this coming age are so wildly expansive in scope that they seem too good to be true, yet integral to Christian faith is the hopeful expectation that such lavish promises will be one day realized. In (over)reaction to idealism, cynicism adopts an attitude that seems unshaped by the hope of one day hearing the voice from the throne crying out "Behold, I am making all things new" (Revelation 21:5).

So when will God make all things right? When will dystopia give way to utopia? Idealists answer with now, cynics with never, but the hopeful realists among us answer with "already, but not yet." The astounding teaching of the New Testament is that the long-awaited future age of new creation is reserved not just for the future; by virtue of Jesus' resurrection the new age is leaping backward from tomorrow and into today! We will revisit this again in the closing chapter, but for now it is important to know that Jews in Jesus' day acknowledged two distinct "ages" or epochs of salvation history. The present age is marked by evil and oppression, but the eschatological "age to come" will be inaugurated by the great Day of the LORD and characterized by peace and salvation.[13] When Jesus came preaching that "the kingdom of God is at hand" (Mark 1:15; cf. Matthew 4:17), he was making the shocking announcement that the eschatological reign of God, so anticipated by the prophets, was suddenly afoot in his ministry. But in his first coming, Jesus did not consummate this reign. He did not introduce an idealistic era in which all illnesses are stopped and death is finalized. Nor did he promise that with the right amount of faith and effort we can somehow redeem ourselves and the world, and bring about in our own power the transformation for which we pine. This final consummation awaits his *second* coming.

In the meantime, we use the language of "already, but not yet." This understanding of time recasts our anthropology because, as Paul teaches us, in Christ we are "new creations" (2 Corinthians 5:17; Galatians 6:15; cf. Ephesians 4:24; Colossians 3:10), language corresponding with the age to come, yet we still "groan inwardly" along with creation as we await the full arrival of that eschatological age (Romans 8:23). And although creation groans, it is groaning in the direction of the renewal assured by the resurrection (the clearest harbinger of the coming new age) and by the subsequent colonization of rebirthed human beings as "new creations" in its midst. New creation awaits, but it is somehow underway even now.

The resetting of our eschatological clocks means that we are not just living post-Eden and pre-parousia, but in the awkward overlap of the ages. To the question When will God make all things right? the biblical answer is not the idealists' now or the cynics' never, but the hopeful realists' already, but not yet.

DISCUSSION QUESTIONS

1. When were some of your own idealist expectations dashed? How did you respond?

2. Give an example of idealistic theology you have been taught that does not hold up in real-life struggle and experience?

3. Where are you most likely to be an idealist, in anthropology (by overestimating your abilities and importance), in cosmology (by denying the evil and fallenness of our world) or in theology (by assuming that God will not allow hardship)? *where we want to land*

4. According to the author, hopeful realists emphasize the "already, but not yet" character of biblical eschatology. Name one way you see God already making things right and new, and name one way you know he is not yet finished with re-creation.

religiosity

The greatest work project of the
ancient world is a story of disaster.
The unexcelled organization and
enormous energy that were concentrated in
building the Tower of Babel resulted in such a
shattered community and garbled communication
that civilization is still trying to recover. Effort, even if the effort is
religious (perhaps especially when the effort is religious), does not in
itself justify anything.

—Eugene Peterson, *A Long Obedience in the Same Direction*

Prayer must never be seen as carrying out a program, fulfilling a quota.

—Hans Urs von Balthasar, *Prayer*

*But woe to you Pharisees! For you tithe mint and rue and every herb,
and neglect justice and the love of God.*

Luke 11:42

BRIAN AND POLISH WINE—LEGALISTIC SELF-DENIAL

I was sitting in a church in Poland with a mission team of Baptist college students. Next to me was Brian. In my years as a campus minister, I had met few students with such passionate zeal for Christ. I was excited about the upcoming week of ministry at his side in Warsaw.

An exchange of glances between the student team members in front of us conveyed that the Communion cup traveling down the pews was filled with real wine. There was a nudge to my right. Brian had scribbled a message on a small piece of paper: "Don't want to offend anyone, but I can't take Communion." Thus began a hurried, clandestine passing of notes during the passing of the cup.

"Why not?" I wrote in response.

"It's real wine."

"So?"

"Alcohol has never touched my lips." The conflict in his conscience was intensifying as the cup drew ever closer to our aisle.

"What a great first time this will be—wine symbolic of Christ's blood, served on the field of mission service." The cup was now on our row.

"But I have been pure all my life." Hmm . . .

"You are not 'pure' because of abstinence. You are 'pure' only because you have been cleansed by the blood that wine represents."

I passed the note to Brian as someone passed the cup to me. When I was finished, I offered the blood of Christ to my dear brother with a warm smile.

He took his first sip of alcohol.

SPIRITUAL ACTIVITY ≠ SPIRITUALITY

I was keenly sensitive to Brian's torment of soul during that tense eucharistic moment because I was a legalist in recovery. For much of my life I understood Christianity as the successful performance of certain dos and the successful abstinence from certain don'ts. Self-denial resulted in spiritual merits. Spiritual activity amounted to "spirituality."

We regularly hear people say that when they awake and begin the day with a good quiet time, then everything about that day is just so much better. They feel supernaturally infused with vigor. There is a spiritual zing to their step. The day's events seem to more providentially fall into place. When we reflect back on our week and realize how many Bible studies we have attended, how many concerned phone calls we've made, how many chapters we have devoured in the latest devotional bestseller, then we tend to experience a certain sense of satisfaction, a sense of spiritual well-being, a sense of divine pleasure and approval.

But is this sense of satisfaction due to spending intimate time lovingly interacting with our Lord, or could it be due to something else, something that may even be grossly offensive to him?

I used to meet regularly with a dear friend on Friday mornings for accountability and mutual encouragement in ministry. He is a gifted Bible teacher and diligently devoted to the mission of Christ among the youth and college subculture. I was continually sharpened and challenged through our time together in these weekly meetings. Then on one glorious, sunshine-bathed day when God's smiling radiance was cast out across the sky and everything below it, I was anticipating one of these scheduled meetings when I suddenly suffered an abrupt pang of anxiety that darkened my otherwise bright world. It was that feeling we get when we realize an hour before class that the assignment we never began is due, that the project deadline is today and we are not prepared for the boardroom presentation. I found myself quickly taking spiritual inventory of my day in response to this twinge of anxiety: *Had I spent time in prayer and study this morning?*

For a brief moment my spiritual status was hanging in the balance. Then, with a sigh of relief, I realized that I had spent *extra* time that morning in prayer and that I had been fairly regular in my Scripture reading throughout the week. I breathed a deep sigh of relief, and once again the day was basking in sunlight under the approving smile of God.

Until I was hit with something else rather suddenly—a severe dose of conviction. God had allowed my wheels to mentally spin over all this for a brief moment before confronting me with just how revolting my line of reasoning was. The cathartic happiness I momentarily enjoyed when I realized that I had indeed performed well with an extended, extra-credit quiet time that day was, in reality, a false happiness founded on the dangerous notion that my spirituality is based on spiritual performance, that my spiritual standing before God (and people!) is based on my religious achievements. I viewed my morning quiet time as a due paid in sufficient amount to earn me a respectable spiritual platform on which to stand throughout the day.

Let's think carefully about this "good feeling" we get when we know we have spent an entire hour in the presence of God (especially if it is in the early morning!), interceding for his church and studying his Scriptures. Does that sense of euphoria arise from encountering our Lord or from some sick sense of spiritual accomplishment? Are we feeling good about God or about ourselves and our laudable spiritual performance of the day? Are we delighted with the relational access God has graciously permitted us, or are we delighted with the false sense of self-assurance we find in adding another notch to our religious belts?

Legalism is the attempt to gain spiritual standing before God by keeping religious rules. When legalists have achieved and performed according to the established expectations, they assume their religious obligations have been fulfilled. This performance-based approach to religious life spawns *religiosity, moralism, ritualism*—words used to designate empty spiritual activity practiced by rote and for the purpose of impressing, not worshiping.

God's disapproval of empty or wrongly motivated religious practices is vividly sketched throughout the Bible. Nadab and Abihu offered "unauthorized" fire in the wilderness (Numbers 3:4). Saul offered an illegitimate sacrifice when Samuel did not show up in time (1 Samuel 13:8-15). During the final decades of the monarchy, the fidelity of God's people was plausibly maintained on the surface through religious practices, yet their hearts were afoul with spiritual rot. To such a religiously active people God cried out through the prophet's lips:

> I hate, I despise your feasts,
> and I take no delight in your solemn assemblies.
> Even though you offer me your burnt offerings and grain
> offerings,
> I will not accept them;
> and the peace offerings of your fattened animals,
> I will not look upon them.
> Take away from me the noise of your songs;
> to the melody of your harps I will not listen.
> But let justice roll down like waters,
> and righteousness like an ever-flowing stream. (Amos
> 5:21-24; see also Isaiah 1:11-17; Jeremiah 6:20; 7:21-24)

God's words through Amos may seem harsh, but the same furious sentiments reverberate throughout the Gospels from the lips of Jesus: "Woe to you Pharisees! For you tithe mint and rue and every herb, and neglect justice and the love of God" (Luke 11:42). The religious leaders who ultimately sent Jesus to his brutal death on a Roman cross were expert religionists. Yet their exterior religiosity blinded them so thoroughly that they could try Jesus for blasphemy and assume they were doing God a favor. Religiosity is so powerfully deluding that it can lead us to kill under presumed divine sanction: "the hour is coming when whoever kills you will think he is offering service to God" (John 16:2).

So, it is possible to religiously excel yet ethically fail. We can worship God with our lips while are hearts are far from him (Isaiah 29:13). *When we think we are most* spiritual *before God may actually be when we are most* offensive *to God.*

Religiosity yields the deceiving self-assurance that we are good little boys and girls when we go to church and have our quiet times. Our frenzied spiritual activity makes us feel safe from God, as though we have sufficiently appeased him by fulfilling religious duties. The problem, of course, is that nothing commends us favorably before God other than the redeeming work of Christ crucified, Christ resurrected and Christ ascended—"you come with empty hands or you don't come at all."[1]

When the veil of self-deception is ripped off and we discover the extent to which legalism and religiosity has motivated our entire walk with Christ, it can be painfully disillusioning. This is portrayed with moving literary power by Victor Hugo in his character development of Javert, a major antagonist in *Les Misérables* and one of the most tragic legalists in Western literature. After a lifetime of rigorous devotion to legal duty, an unmerited display of mercy from the ex-convict Jean Valjean collides against everything Javert has ever known—how could a criminal exhibit such remarkable compassion by sparing his pursuer's life? Seeing this "tear in the eye of the law," Javert suffered "the derailment of a soul, the crushing of a probity irresistibly hurled in a straight line and breaking up against God."[2] The exposure of our empty moralism can prove devastating.

So how should we respond to the disillusioning discovery of religiosity and legalism within ourselves and the church? The way the cynical Christian responds is usually with something called "antinomianism."

BRETT AND PERSIAN TOBACCO—CYNICAL ANTINOMIANISM

Within a year of that mission trip to Warsaw when Brian drank Polish wine, I decided to organize a small retreat for the young men I was working with as a campus minister. I sent out an e-mail with the logistical details, announced the discussion topics and mentioned that afterward we could smoke pipes or cigars if they had them. On the day of the retreat, one of the guys planning to join us ran into Brett, the most notorious cynic on campus. When Brett asked the guy about his evening plans, he replied, "I'm going to spend the evening smoking with the campus minister" (not exactly the language of my original advertisement).

The first time Brett deigned to attend a campus ministry event, he wore a T-shirt with this emblazoned across his chest:

Just because God spoke out of Balaam's ass
doesn't mean he wants to speak out of yours.

You get the picture. I suppose the opportunity to smoke with a minister seemed edgy and scandalous enough that he decided to join us, and he was by no means the only cynic who loaded into the vans that evening for the retreat.

A few months earlier I had e-mailed a friend of mine who was working in the Middle East to ask that he keep his eyes open for a good deal on a pipe. Not long after I sent the e-mail, a large box arrived on my doorstep with Arabic postage. Within the mysterious packaging was a hookah, that odd smoking contraption that the caterpillar used in *Alice in Wonderland*. It has a glass water container, a tall neck and a long tube through which the tobacco is smoked. I brought it to the men's retreat as a surprise.

I have never been considered "cool" before—something I made peace with a long time ago. But this status briefly changed after our time of prayer and Bible study at the men's retreat when I removed the hookah from its curious case. Its sudden unveiling was met with wondrous gawking. There it stood, shimmering in exotic, Persian splendor. *You've gotta be kidding. The campus minister has a hookah?* None were more exhilarated than Brett, the cynic whose rebellious desire to smoke with the campus minister had brought him into our ranks.

The primary attraction of the hookah for these young men, however, was not the pleasant smoking experience it could afford. The attraction was sourced in the notion that the presence of such a controversial device at a ministry event was *rebellious*. It appeared to be a protest against legalistic decrees. There was a euphoric sense of triumph when the hookah appeared because we were going to "stick it to the man" and smoke the cool Persian thing, an act that surely would have scandalized all our former Sunday school teachers.

And then we realized that I left some of the parts at home. Oh well.

Antinomianism derives from the Greek prefix *anti* (against) and the Greek word *nomos* (law). Literally, the term means "against law."

Whereas legalists keep the expected religious regulations, anti-nomians buck up against all the rules. The hookah was alluring because it was rebellious. Smoking it would effect a minor mutiny against the system.

During my early seminary years it suddenly felt cool to drink a beer, smoke a pipe and say a cussword every now and then while preparing for vocational ministry. For those of us who grew up in the Bible belt, these are stereotypical no-nos. The legalism nurtured and reinforced by years of church life can sometimes appear so ridiculous that we begin to rebel against certain religious taboos in the name of "Christian freedom." But if we decide to break a taboo by drinking a beer, is our primary pleasure in the taste of a beverage God enables us to enjoy or in the distance from the established church that draining its dregs effects?

Clearly, legalism is wrong. But the antinomianism of the Christian cynic is an overreaction. In avoiding legalism, we may find ourselves not just breaking ridiculous taboos (like smoking a hookah), but actually committing sin under the banner of "Christian freedom" (like smoking a hookah with illegal substances). In avoiding empty spiritual activity, many Christian cynics embrace spiritual apathy or even worse, a flagrant antinomianism that purposefully seeks to break biblical principles and to fail valid expectations.

SELF-RIGHTEOUS LEGALISM VERSUS RIGHTEOUS OBEDIENCE

The Bible may rail against *self-righteous legalism*, but it certainly demands *righteous obedience*. The line between the two is exquisitely fine (most of the slopes the Christian must walk are of the slippery variety). Thankfully, we are guided by the indwelling presence of One who knows the terrain.

This may sound suspicious, but there was a time in my life when God seemed to be instructing me to pray less. We usually envision God with his arms crossed and impatiently tapping his foot in frustration over our lack of devotion to spiritual disciplines. But my own spiritual activity had become so fraught with performance-based legalism that I needed to learn how to believe God loved me even when I did not spend an hour in prayer each day like a good little boy. I had been striving for so long to bring him something spiritually impressive enough to earn that precious pronouncement, "You are my beloved child, with whom I am well pleased" (see Mark 1:11).

God, however, was already making that pronouncement. I just lacked the ears to hear. So he instituted a sabbath of sorts for my spiritual activity. The warning of Eugene Peterson was appropriate to my situation:

> If there is no Sabbath—no regular and commanded not-working, not-talking—we soon become totally absorbed in what we are doing and saying, and God's work is either forgotten or marginalized. When we work, we are most god-like, which means that it is in our work that it is easiest to develop god-pretensions. Unsabbathed, our work becomes the entire context in which we define our lives. We lose God-consciousness, God-awareness, sightings of resurrection. We lose the capacity to sing "This is my Father's World" and end up chirping little self-centered ditties about what *we* are doing and feeling.[3]

I was in need of instituting a "sabbath" in my practice of spiritual disciplines because at some point I had begun to equate spirituality with spiritual activity. In my performance-based activity of religious achievement, I had subtly begun to exalt myself, not my Lord. Once again, when we think we are most *spiritual* before God may actually be when we are most *offensive* to God.

This strange new season of limited quiet times was an attempt at disentangling the religiosity out of my relationship with God. But I should note that this season did not last long. I soon became aware that it was time to hit the floor again with my knees and open the Bible with fresh new vigor.

It is true that many believers attend church, listen to Christian music, practice spiritual disciplines or share the gospel because they are hoping to etch extra notches in their religious belts. The number of memorized verses and hours spent reading the Bible can easily become merit badges sewn onto an external religious canvas beneath which is nothing more than empty self-righteousness. But we *are* called to faithful obedience, to sincere acts of kindness and compassion. Spiritual disciplines are easily sabotaged by merit-based religiosity, but this does not license us to discard them in antinomian zeal as legalistic debris from institutional religion. By embracing a sabbath in my practice of spiritual disciplines, God was training me to discern the fine line between self-righteous legalism and righteous devotion.

Complex traditions inform where we tend to draw this fine line. Pietistic genes are in our spiritual DNA, pressuring us into the regular (and sometimes rote) performance of religious activities. But other genes have given us a hypersensitivity to any notion of "doing" or "working." Scripture calls us to an unapologetic tension between the two. We see this tension in Paul's instructions in Philippians—"Work out your own salvation in fear and trembling, for it is God who works in you, both to will and to work for his good pleasure" (Philippians 2:12-13). Though God is the ultimate source of the labor that ensures our salvation, we are nonetheless exhorted to work. This tension between our work and God's work becomes strikingly clear when holding up one of Paul's most famed slogans along with one of James's most (unfairly) infamous slogans:

A person is not justified by works of the law but through faith in Jesus Christ. (Galatians 2:16)

You see that a person is justified by works and not by faith alone. (James 2:24)

Though canonical tension can be disturbing at times (I am referring to the apparent diversity between different sections of Scripture), it often proves extremely helpful. However these two texts are to be read, it is certain that we cannot comfortably place ourselves among the legalists or the antinomians.

Another passage that helps us navigate between self-righteous legalism and righteous obedience is Titus 2:11-14. Here, grace is cele-

brated not only for "bringing salvation for all people" but also for
"training us to renounce ungodliness and worldly passions, and to live
self-controlled, upright, and godly lives." Those of us in the Protestant
tradition are quite familiar with grace's role of bringing salvation, but
less familiar with the notion that grace *trains* us for ethical living. The
Greek verb behind *training* is *paideuō*, which can connote sharp disci-
pline (it sometimes means to "whip" or "scourge").[4] We are not just
saved by grace but forcefully motivated by grace to live disciplined lives
that are pleasing to the One who graciously saves us. So grace excludes
self-righteous religiosity yet demands righteous obedience.

DISCUSSION QUESTIONS

1. Share a time in your life when you had plenty of "spiritual activity"
   even though your relationship with Christ was plagued with sin or
   stagnation?

2. What is a religious practice in your life that could easily cause you
   to become spiritually prideful.

3. How would you feel if God asked you to take a break from some of
   your most faithfully practiced spiritual activities? Or are you unable to name one because of your own antinomian tendencies?

4. Is there a spiritual activity that you once practiced regularly that
   you rarely or no longer practice now? Why the change?

5. Is there anything you do (or do *not* do) in the name of "Christian
   freedom"? What are your motives?

5   experientialism

*As we ought not to reject and
condemn all affections, as though true
religion did not at all consist in them; so, on
the other hand, we ought not to approve of all,
as though everyone that was religiously affected had
true grace, and was therein the subject of the saving
influences of the Spirit of God.*

—Jonathan Edwards, *A Treatise Concerning Religious Affections*

*Experience must never be the criterion of truth; truth must always be
the criterion of experience.*

—John R. W. Stott, *Baptism & Fullness*

*Today many confuse "spirituality" with "experience"—the unintentional
result being that they actually worship human esoteric moments or
points of wonder, without apprehending the fuller reality that God has
in store for us.*

—Edith Humphrey, *Ecstasy and Intimacy*

ASCENTS

I had a severe inferiority complex regarding my spirituality for several months during college. Friends were beginning to see strange visions during prayer and were moved to tears during worship. I was spending hours in prayer and seeing nothing extraordinary and attending the same worship services but with no tears of my own to show for it. I wondered what was wrong with me.

Rumors trickled southward that something divine was afoot in Canada called the "Toronto Blessing." It was reported that people were being so overwhelmed with the presence of God that they burst out uncontrollably in "holy laughter." This is what I was looking for, not so much laughter per se, but some palpable experience of the sublime power of God's Spirit. When I heard that one of the ministers associated with those Toronto churches was leading a conference just seven hours away, some friends and I organized a pilgrimage. We would ascend northward to Kentucky, where I hoped to find a landmark flash, zap, bang moment that would usher us into the next level of spiritual maturity.

During the opening worship service the main speaker charged everyone who wanted to experience the power of the Holy Spirit to come forward for prayer. I heard the "holy laughter" in the chapel and watched bodies collapse to the floor from being "slain in the Spirit" as the Toronto prayer team placed their hands on those who came forward. Courageously casting off the inhibiting fetters of my very non-charismatic upbringing, I ventured out for prayer. Whatever God had for me, I wanted it.

I lifted my arms high in the air as someone placed his hand on my head to pray for me. The prayer was passionate and moving, but then I realized that he was pushing on my forehead, as if trying to knock me down.

So this is how it works? I wondered.

I did not come all the way from Georgia for some charismatic Canadian to knock me to the floor. I was more than willing to be "slain in the Spirit," but I told the Lord right then and there that if I was going down, he was going to have to do the knocking. So this fellow and I entered a contest of sorts, him pressing my forehead with his hand while I arched my back against his pressure. Finally, the poor guy just gave up on me and, I guess, went to someone else more receptive. I was left standing there upright and erect, amidst the sounds of holy laughter, my hands desperately outstretched to heaven for something that never came.

This *non*-experience precipitated a gradual descent into disillusionment with the mysticism associated with the more charismatic/Pentecostal dimensions of Christianity.

A few years later I made another ascent. This time it was up a series of staircases to the hallowed upper levels of Beeson Divinity School where our faculty prayerfully studied and prepared for their lectures. I wasn't necessarily looking for a supernatural encounter this time, but I needed *something*, something tangible, something I could hold onto as I struggled with what Martyn Lloyd-Jones called "spiritual depression."[1]

The man I sought on this day to bring relief to this inconsolable discouragement was my preaching professor. My respect for Dr. Robert Smith was (and is still) immense—I knew he spent more time praying for his students than grading their work (the latter perhaps necessitated the former). I knew him to be a wise and caring brother before whom I could bear my heart and then receive warm, sensitive encouragement.

He offered me a chair, and then the dam burst as soon as I opened my mouth to speak. The pain and confusion of my internal turmoil spewed unchecked all over his desk and office floor. How thankful I was for such open ears.

And then he interrupted me.

We are not supposed to do that. When someone is pouring out their wounded heart, we don't interrupt them, especially when there is at least a hint of depression going on. We are supposed to listen attentively and carefully, maybe even take some notes and occasionally nod to indicate interest. This beloved professor spent hours every day listening to young seminarians preach their first sermons. He could sit with patience and attentiveness through anything. But right there in mid-sentence he interrupted my pathetic babbling with this question:

"Do you hear what *word* you keep using?"

I had used a lot of words and was in the process of trying to get out a few more. What one word was he talking about?

"You keep using the word *feel*."

Pause.

He seemed to have said this as though it were an indictment of sorts.

I kept pausing.

The emotionally distraught monologue hanging on my lips could not materialize in the face of his observation. The tirade was instantly cut short with the realization that something was askew in my understanding of spirituality. As I gradually made the ascent out of my state of depression, however, I was also making a descent of sorts into disillusionment with feelings and emotions.

When distrust in the supernatural and emotional elements of Christian faith arises, we begin edging into cynicism. It is hard not to be cynical when you find out that the superspiritual guy who was supposedly "baptized in the Spirit" last month just got his girlfriend pregnant. It is hard not to be cynical when you see someone weeping in misery over their sin, only to realize their emotional remorse is more related to his or her disappointment in getting caught than in the pain they've caused others. As we will see, experiential spirituality is extremely dangerous, but in turn we will find that the cynical aversion to emotions and the supernatural is also dangerous.

THE SPIRITUALITY BUILT ON EXPERIENCES: STITCHING SUMMIT TO SUMMIT

Experiential spirituality measures Christian maturity on the basis of mystical encounters and emotional feelings. Healthy spirituality is therefore *felt* spirituality. A good quiet time is one that is *not* quiet, when we *hear* God's voice and *feel* his presence. Conversely, a "dry time" signifies disobedience or spiritual regression. Those who experience apocalyptic visions are accorded a higher spiritual rank than those who pray in the face of divine silence. A sermon is "good" when it is followed by a dramatic response; a sermon is "bad" when everyone casually leaves for Sunday-afternoon lunch without shedding a tear.

When we speak of mountain-top experiences, we are normally referring to those defining moments when God is so tangibly real to us, when our attention before him is so rapt and when his voice seems so clear. Mountain-top spirituality is when our relationship with God is only enjoyed from the perch of grand vistas towering above the obscuring cloud line.

As a campus minister I have required students to write out their testimonies on various applications for mission trips or for leadership teams. There were certainly unique elements, but so many of these personal narratives shared a basic story line that went something like this:

> I gave my life to Christ when I was very young at Vacation Bible School [or through a revival meeting or a worship service, perhaps]. But I didn't really understand my faith at all until I went on a youth group retreat several years later. After the retreat, though, I kinda fell into the wrong crowd [or maybe, started dating this guy/girl] and was led astray. I didn't think much about God until a friend invited me to go to a youth camp one summer in high school. After that camp God really convicted me so I rededicated my life and started growing again in my faith. By the end of the summer, though, I was going back to my old ways and I kinda just forgot about God. Then some friends talked me into going on a missions trip during my senior year and ever since then I've been really excited about Jesus and I just want to serve him!

These testimonials came primarily from college freshmen who had been reared in the church. Their spiritual histories could be traced from one event (VBS, retreat, camp, missions trip, etc.) to another.

But a healthy Christian life cannot be stitched together from a series of disjointed mountain-top experiences. We need a Christian spirituality that endures the shadowy, low-lying valleys and the rocky slopes in between all those glorious summits.

We must not discredit or avoid mountain-top experiences, however. They are certainly biblical—just think of Moses receiving the law on Mount Sinai, Elijah calling down fire from Mount Carmel, the Israelites celebrating festivals on Mount Zion, and Jesus being glorified on the Mount of Transfiguration. We must acknowledge, though, that our path will wind through "the valley of the shadow of death" (Psalm 23:4), and some mountain-top experiences will not be so enjoyable. Moses may have spoken with God "face to face" on Mount Sinai (Exodus 33:11; cf. Deuteronomy 34:10), but his life mournfully ended on Mount Nebo, where he saw the land whose flowing milk and honey he would never taste. Elijah may have been triumphant on Mount Carmel, but soon afterward he was found scared and dejected on Mount Horeb (Sinai), where God was not in the strong wind, the earthquake or the fire. The Israelites may have joyfully sung those Songs of Ascents while climbing Mount Zion at Passover. But those slopes were also scaled one day by Babylonians who came to besiege and destroy. Jesus radiated in holy splendor on the Mount of Transfiguration, but he died naked and scorned on Calvary's hill.

Mystical encounters and emotional feelings are certainly a part of Christianity. It must be remembered, however, that there is nothing distinctively "Christian" in feeling and experiencing the numinous: "All that is 'spiritual' is not holy."[2] For the rest of this chapter we will sort through both biblical affirmations and biblical admonitions of experientialism and then consider how a wholesale rejection of extraordinary experiences is a dangerous overreaction on behalf of cynical skeptics.

EMOTIONAL EXPERIENCES AND SPIRITUALITY:
"JUST FOLLOW YOUR HEART"

When my children were born I shed tears of joy. When my grandparents died, I shed tears of grief. When I hear about an act of child abuse, I get angry. When I preach on God's power and love, I get excited. When my toddler son tries to do a cartwheel, I laugh. Emotions are integral to human existence. God made us this way, and he is repeatedly presented in Scripture as an emotional being:

> My heart recoils within me;
>> my compassion grows warm and tender. (Hosea 11:8)

> In the fire of his jealousy,
>> all the earth shall be consumed. (Zephaniah 1:18)

> When Jesus saw her weeping, and the Jews who had come with her also weeping, he was deeply moved in his spirit and greatly troubled. And he said, "Where have you laid him?" They said to him, "Lord, come and see." Jesus wept. (John 11:33-35)

> And [Jesus] looked around at them with anger, grieved at their hardness of heart. (Mark 3:5)

> Do not grieve the Holy Spirit of God. (Ephesians 4:30; cf. Isaiah 63:10)[3]

God is emotional, and we are made in his image, so emotions are essential to our interaction with him. There is legitimately "a time to weep, and a time to laugh; a time to mourn, and a time to dance" (Ecclesiastes 3:4). Consider David "leaping and dancing before the Lord" as the ark approached Jerusalem (2 Samuel 6:16). Consider the aching tears and the joyous exclamations throughout the Psalms. Consider the internal agony of Jesus in Gethsemane. Consider Paul's repeated command to the Philippian church to "rejoice in the Lord always" (Philippians 4:4). The Bible encourages emotional responses to and interactions with God.[4]

But the Bible discourages an imbalanced reliance on our emotional feelings and impulses. In acknowledging that feelings are important and helpful in many regards, Eugene Peterson bluntly writes that "they tell me next to nothing about God or my relation to God."[5] In a chapter titled "True Religion Is Not Feeling but Willing," A. W. Tozer writes, "The emotional life is a proper and noble part of the total per-

sonality, but it is, by its very nature, of secondary importance."[6] Every
part of who we are has been corrupted by the Fall. Our emotions are
not a neutral realm—they have not escaped sin's distorting effects
and must not be fully trusted.

A regularly dispensed piece of advice among Christians today is
"just follow your heart." Yet God warns the Israelites "not to follow
after your own heart" (Numbers 15:39; cf. 1 Kings 12:33), and in Jeremiah we hear him say that "the heart is deceitful above all things, /
and desperately sick; / who can understand it?" (Jeremiah 17:9). A few
chapters earlier, God addressed Judah as "evil people . . . who stub-
bornly follow their own heart" (Jeremiah 13:10; cf. Jeremiah 23:17).
Our emotions are prone to ungodly tendencies and should be viewed
with a healthy degree of suspicion.

Experiential spirituality often assumes that feelings or sensations
directly result from contact with God. But we are complex beings,
and emotions are also connected to neurological processes firing in
our brains and to hormones that are released from our glands. Emotions can fluctuate from factors related to our life stage, to the weather
or even to what we ate for breakfast. Feelings can be as much physio-
logical as spiritual.

It should also be acknowledged that some of us are just more "emotional" than others. Certain personality types are less prone to express themselves in emotional ways. Experiential spirituality places
such emphasis on emotional expression that those with less passionate personality types are regarded as spiritually inferior. I have found,
however, that those who seem devoid of emotion often walk more
consistently with Christ than those of us with more emotional dispositions![7]

So even though we are called to relate to God emotionally, we
must not place too much emphasis on how we feel (or on how we
do not feel) in determining our spiritual health. Our emotions can
be innocently misplaced or even sinfully distorted. It is even possible that we can find our emotions blindly *opposite* to what God
desires:

In that day the Lord GOD of hosts
called for *weeping* and mourning; . . .
and behold, *joy and gladness.* (Isaiah 22:12-13, emphasis added)

SPIRITUAL EXPERIENCES AND SPIRITUALITY: "IS SAUL AMONG THE PROPHETS?"

God is emotional, and he is also explicitly supernatural. The Gospel of John tells us that "God is spirit" (John 4:24), so he will inevitably manifest himself at times in supernatural ways. Innumerable examples of these (sometimes bizarre!) manifestations appear in Scripture. Balaam's donkey opened his mouth and spoke; fire did not consume the bush that caught Moses' attention; fire did consume the altar Elijah had soaked with water; a virgin Jewish girl found herself pregnant with the Messiah; the Holy Spirit gave voice to the gospel in multiple languages on Pentecost; Philip was instantly translocated from one region to another; Paul, it seems, ecstatically found himself in the "third heaven" (2 Corinthians 12:2). The list could go on. In interacting with us, God will at times stretch the boundaries of nature and reveal himself in moving, dramatic fashion.

This should be welcome among us, but not without necessary warnings and admonitions.

1. Spiritual experiences can be as much occultic as holy. Along with our emotional feelings, spiritual experiences must be assessed with great caution. There are other spirits besides the Holy Spirit:[8] "Beloved, do not believe every spirit, but test the spirits to see whether they are from God, for many false prophets have gone out into the world" (1 John 4:1). There are accounts throughout the Bible describing spiritual experiences and supernatural manifestations that God is *not* the source of. When Aaron threw down Moses' staff on Pharaoh's court, it became a serpent by the power of God, but the Egyptian sorcerers were able to produce the same miraculous sign (although we should recall that Moses' serpent *did* devour the others). These same magicians were also able to turn water into blood and to conjure up frogs, mimicking the first two plagues.

Some forty years later Moses warned the Israelites on the plains of
Moab against following prophets and visionaries who could perform
supernatural wonders:

> If a prophet or a *dreamer of dreams* arises among you and gives
> you a sign or a wonder, and the *sign or wonder* that he tells you
> comes to pass, and if he says, "Let us go after other gods," which
> you have not known, "and let us serve them," you shall not lis-
> ten to the words of that prophet or that dreamer of dreams. For
> the LORD your God is testing you, to know whether you love the
> LORD your God with all your heart and with all your soul. (Deu-
> teronomy 13:1-3, emphasis added)

Experiential spirituality is quick to validate the authority of spiritual leaders on the basis of their ability to perform signs and wonders.
This passage from Deuteronomy demonstrates that it is possible to be
spiritually powerful but theologically wrong, and therefore dangerous
to God's people. Someone's theology is much more qualifying for leadership than their ability to display or manipulate the supernatural.

Misleading demonstrations of spiritual power are also found in the
New Testament. Though the apostles performed extraordinary miracles, they encountered others during their ministries who amazed
people with supernatural abilities. While preaching the gospel in Samaria, Philip and Peter encountered a man named Simon

> who had previously practiced magic in the city and amazed the
> people of Samaria, saying that he himself was somebody great.
> They all paid attention to him, from the least to the greatest,
> saying, "This man is the power of God that is called Great."
> And they paid attention to him because for a long time he had
> amazed them with his magic. (Acts 8:9-11)

Simon embraced Philip's preaching and was baptized, but old hab-
its die hard—he offered money that he might purchase access to the
power of the Spirit at work through the apostles, an offer that was
refused with great vehemence!

Similarly, Paul had a brief encounter with a Jewish magician in Cyprus who was obviously gifted with supernatural abilities but tried to turn the local proconsul away from embracing the gospel message (Acts 13:4-12). Later in Macedonia the apostle ran into a group of people that profited from fortune-telling. The success of their craft was due to a "spirit of divination" that influenced one of their servants (Acts 16:16).

Jesus warned his disciples that "false christs and false prophets will arise and perform signs and wonders, to lead astray, if possible, the elect" (Mark 13:22; cf. Matthew 24:24). An inordinate fascination with the extraordinary and the miraculous makes us susceptible to the deceptive misguidance of God's greatest enemies. The misleading power of spiritual experiences was immediately seen among some of the earliest churches. It is explicitly clear in Revelation that the power to produce signs and wonders is part of the arsenal of pagan leaders and demonic spirits (see Revelation 13:13-15; 16:14). Reliance on dreams is criticized in Jude 8, and in Colossae some believers were under the spell of a teacher (or group of teachers) promoting senseless asceticism, encouraging the worship of angelic beings and reveling in visions: "Let no one disqualify you, insisting on asceticism and worship of angels, going on in detail about visions, puffed up without reason by his sensuous mind" (Colossians 2:18). These examples (and there are many more) evidence the frightening reality that spiritual experiences can be as much *occultic* as *holy*.

2. There are invalid responses to valid spiritual experiences. Even when God *is* the source of mystical encounters or supernatural manifestations, we may respond to them inappropriately. Paul ended up with the "thorn" in his flesh because he had experienced an epiphany so grand that God had to debilitate him to prevent the response of spiritual pride: "To keep me from becoming conceited because of these surpassingly great revelations, there was given me a thorn in my flesh, a messenger of Satan, to torment me" (2 Corinthians 12:7 NIV).

The Corinthians had been guilty themselves of responding inappropriately to God's supernatural power. Proponents of experientialism place considerable attention on 1 Corinthians 12–14, the lengthiest material in the Bible on "spiritual gifts." It must be remembered, though, that Paul is writing to correct the Corinthians' response to their corporate experiences of the Spirit. In spite of their active operation in spiritual gifts, Paul writes in 1 Corinthians 3:1: "I . . . could not address you as spiritual people, but as people of the flesh." We can practice spiritual gifts and yet be unspiritual. There are no legitimate grounds for denying that these gifts are valid for contemporary church life, but it is important to note that the primary reason we know about spiritual gifts from Scripture is because a first-century church was practicing them inappropriately.[9]

Along with spiritual pride, another inappropriate response to the miraculous found in Scripture is the misuse of its power. The reason Moses died on Mount Nebo, forbidden to enter the Promised Land, was because he struck that rock at Meribah-kadesh with his staff rather than spoke to it as God had commanded (Numbers 20:2-13; cf. Deuteronomy 32:48-52). In another wilderness scene centuries later, Jesus was tempted by Satan to utilize legitimate spiritual power in an illegitimate way (Matthew 4:1-11; Luke 4:1-13). Turning those stones into bread would not have honored his Father or helped his mission.

3. Valid spiritual experiences do not necessarily validate our spirituality. There was a saying that circulated among God's people during the early days of the monarchy: "Is Saul also among the prophets?" (1 Samuel 10:12; 19:24). After he was anointed to become king by the prophet Samuel, Saul ran into a group of prophets at Gibeah and he began prophesying with them, to the surprise of those who had known him previously (and to Saul himself, it seems). This strange experience validated Saul as God's anointed leader over his people. But some years later, after "the Spirit of the LORD departed from" him (1 Samuel 16:14), Saul maliciously sent some cronies to capture David, who had found refuge among the prophets at Naioth. When Saul's entourage showed up, they suddenly began prophesying! This happened to all three delegations Saul sent to Naioth until finally he came down himself "and the Spirit of God came upon him also, and as he went he prophesied" (1 Samuel 19:23). For the entire day and night, the king of Israel, with David's murder as his agenda, was found continually prophesying in Naioth. This was by no means a validation of Saul's spirituality.

The Saul story provides a prime example of God displaying his supernatural power through people *in spite of* their spirituality and not *because of* their spirituality. Balaam is another example, of course. What may be more shocking than God's speaking through a donkey is that he chose to speak through Balaam, a pagan prophet-for-hire who had no real vested interest in serving the purposes of Israel's God. Valid spiritual experiences do not necessarily indicate spiritual maturity.

In Rowan Williams's *The Wound of Knowledge*, he discusses a list of spiritual experiences penned by St. John of the Cross:

> It is a deliberately devastating catalogue, exhibiting a rare and alarming sensitivity to the risks of self-deception in the spiritual life. The conclusions are stark: no "spiritual" experience whatsoever can provide a clear security, an unambiguous sign of God's favor.[10]

There are many heroic men and women whom God used dramatically in Scripture, but he also used antiheroes like Pharaoh, Nebuchadnezzar, Judas Iscariot and even Satan. If God can supernaturally grant prophecies to Balaam and his donkey, then we need not be overly impressed with those through whom we witness supernatural power today.

BAD PNEUMATOLOGY AND THE "ELITE SPIRITUAL ARISTOCRACY"
Pneumatology refers to our understanding of the Holy Spirit. Sadly, many Christians seem quite content to discuss God the Father and God the Son, but they either remain aloof about God the Spirit or they focus on him to the exclusion of the other two.

Those who are more open to the Spirit's activity and presence often point out that a failure to apprehend God's supernatural capabilities is to put him into a box. The observation is correct! But experiential spirituality suffers from its own misperceptions of God's Spirit. Associating the Spirit's work so strongly with emotional feelings and mystical encounters is to unpack God from one box and cram him into another. Experientialism packages the Spirit in a box that limits his work to that which is sensational, and it often views him as an impersonal force. These misunderstandings can be expressed in the following myths.

1. *The more normal, the less spiritual.* The sending of God's Spirit into the first New Testament church was a boisterous, dramatic scene. Luke tells us in Acts 2 that there was the noisy sound of a "mighty rushing wind" (v. 2) and the startling sight of "tongues as of fire" (v. 3). It is reported that all this happened "suddenly" (v. 2).

If we establish our expectations of the Holy Spirit on Acts 2, then we will understandably assume that the Spirit's work is always sudden and dramatic. The ordinary and mundane will in turn be assigned an inferior status. As my wife one day observed, many of us tend to believe that the more *normal* something is, then the less *spiritual* it is. When something weird or crazy happens in a worship service, then it is assumed that the Spirit was powerfully active. If no one gets worked up, then it is assumed that the Spirit was quenched.

As its namesake indicates, Pentecostalism has taken Pentecost as the prototypical model of the Holy Spirit's activity in the life of the church. Other Christians could learn from this—many mainline denominations seem to forget that the church was born out of a surprising and powerful display of the supernatural! But there is much more to the work of the Spirit in Scripture than what we read in Acts 2, and much of that work is not sudden and dramatic. In John's Gospel, we learn that the Spirit will guide us "into all the truth" (John 16:13)—which is certainly not an overnight endeavor. Paul tells us "we do not know what to pray for as we ought, but the Spirit himself intercedes for us with groanings too deep for words" (Romans 8:26). Do we really notice this subtle activity of divine intercession and groaning? Paul also teaches that "if by the Spirit you put to death the deeds of the body, you will live" (Romans 8:13). This work of transformation by God's Spirit can certainly be sudden and dramatic, but for the most part, it is a slow, ongoing process "from one degree of glory to another" (2 Corinthians 3:18). Rather than instantaneous and flash in the pan, much of the Holy Spirit's work is actually *tedious, painstaking, meticulous, subtle and even, at times, unnoticeable.* Ever heard of Bezalel? When we think of the charismatic heroes in Scripture, he usually does not come to mind, even though he is one of the first people to be explicitly identified as being filled with God's Spirit.[11] His divinely empowered work was not to dramatically part any bodies of water or to prophesy to the congregation. He was filled with the Spirit of God to build stuff. Bezalel was a craftsman, a skilled worker filled with the Spirit to make art. Along with his co-laborer Ohaliab, Bezalel served as the project manager for the construction of the altar, the Ark of the Covenant and the other physical accoutrements of the tabernacle.

> See, I have called by name Bezalel, . . . and I have filled him with the Spirit of God, with ability and intelligence, with knowledge and all craftsmanship, to devise artistic designs, to work in gold, silver, and bronze, in cutting stones for setting, and in carving wood, to work in every craft. (Exodus 31:2-5; cf. Exodus 35:30–36:2)

This description of Bezalel features words rarely associated in contemporary parlance with the work of the Holy Spirit: *ability, intelligence, knowledge, craftsmanship.* His Spirit-filled work was far from sudden or immediately sensational—the chiseling, weaving, engraving and constructing were all meticulous, slow and practical.

To see God only in the sudden, the dramatic and the extraordinary is *sensationalism*, something we find Jesus downplaying throughout the Gospels. He refuses Satan's temptation to cast himself off the temple spire in a crowd-wowing stunt. He tells the Pharisees and Sadducees that "an evil and adulterous nation seeks for a sign" (Matthew 16:4). In the parable of the rich man and Lazarus, the rich man assumes that his brothers will change their ways if they receive warning from someone who has been raised from death. Abraham responds that this sensational plan will not work: "If they do not hear Moses and the Prophets, neither will they be convinced if someone should rise from the dead" (Luke 16:31). After the crucifixion, Thomas had heard the excited resurrection talk, but he vowed not to believe "unless I see in his hands the mark of the nails, and place my hand into his side" (John 20:25). It was just over a week later that the tangibility of the resurrected Christ was thrust right into his face. Thomas professed faith, but here is how Jesus responds: "Have you believed *because you have seen me?* Blessed are those *who have not seen* and yet have believed" (John 20:29, emphasis added).

If we only see the Holy Spirit in the sensational, then we will miss his beautiful work in the tabernacle's embroidery, in a child's gradual grasp of spiritual truth, in a transparent conversation over coffee, and in the faith of those who believe while seeing nothing. During his time at the Genesee monastery, Henri Nouwen wrote of his struggle to discern God in the small, unromantic details of life:

> Maybe I have been living much too fast, too restlessly, too feverishly, forgetting to pay attention to what is happening here and now, right under my nose. Just as a whole world of beauty can be discovered in one flower, so the great grace of God can be tasted in one small moment. Just as no great travels are necessary to see the beauty of creation, so no great ecstasies are needed to discover the love of God. But you have to be still and wait so that you can realize that God is not in the earthquake, the storm, or the lightning, but in the gentle breeze with which he touches your back.[12]

2. The Holy Spirit Is an "It." The earliest seeds of my pneumatology came not from Scripture but from George Lucas. When I saw *Star Wars* as a kid I syncretized that imaginary realm from a long time ago in a galaxy far, far away with my church upbringing to embrace a new vocational assignment: I would become a valiant Jedi for Jesus (that is, *a disciple*), vanquishing evil with my light saber of truth (or *sword of the Spirit*, if you will), skillfully wielding the power of the Force (a.k.a., *Holy Spirit*) to bring justice and goodness to *the remot-*

est part (Acts 1:8 NASB) of the galaxy. I matured out of this vocational aspiration, but I have to confess that it took a while for me to relinquish the fallacious idea that the Holy Spirit corresponds with an impersonal "force." This is the second myth of bad pneumatology that we need to address.

Not too long before I went to that conference in Kentucky during college, I ran into someone I knew quite well, in whom I had invested a great deal of time and energy as he grew in his faith. As we passed by each other on campus, he leaned toward me in clandestine fashion (even though no one was anywhere around) and secretly informed me with a knowing look: "Last night, I got It." I knew he was referring to the Holy Spirit or at least some dramatic experience that signified the receiving of the Holy Spirit.

But what if someone labeled you not as a "him" or a "her," but as an "it"?

The Holy Spirit is a person, not an "it."[13] He is not an impersonal force or power but the third *person* of the Trinity.[14] Depersonalizing the third person of the Trinity not only offends the character of our personal God but promotes our tendency to manipulate him. If we view the Spirit of God as a force or a power, then we are tempted to *wield* and *use* him rather than worship and serve him. This seems to be the attitude of Simon Magus in Acts 8 when he offered cash to Philip and Peter to gain access to their impressive power. The Holy Spirit is "the Spirit of *Christ*" (Romans 8:9; 1 Peter 1:11; cf. Acts 16:7; 2 Corinthians 3:17-18; Philippians 1:19), not the "power" or the "energy" of Christ.[15]

When my friend made the pronouncement that he had gotten "It," there was a bold expression of arrival on his face. It was as though he had just been initiated into some secret order of revved up, superior spirituality. By having gotten "It," he believed himself to have been promoted into the fellowship of the spiritually elite, a fellowship from which some of us felt excluded. In assessing spirituality on the basis of feelings and mystical encounters, experientialism relegates those who lack experiences to a status inferior to what Eugene Peterson calls the "elite spiritual aristocracy."[16]

We have learned that spiritual experiences can lead to spiritual pride. I remember sitting in a Bible study as a college freshman and hearing about the prophecy that Elijah was to one day return and lead a revival among God's people. Suddenly, I was overcome with shock and excitement because, with the authenticating sense of a divine revelation, the thought occurred to me that *I was Elijah*.

(Oh Lord, help us.)

Thankfully, before I could make the self-pronouncement, the Bible study teacher pointed us to the passages where Jesus taught that Elijah had already come as John the Baptist (not as Andy Byers).

I am still so embarrassed by the pathetic, desperate yearning for spiritual significance that led to my audacious assumption that I was Elijah—could there be a more arrogant case of mistaken identity? I know I am not alone, however, in experiencing self-flattering revelations that seem to come from above. On a number of occasions I have heard students describe mystical visions and revelations. Red flags should always be raised if the recipient of the vision is more of the featured "star" than the supposed Giver of the vision. The divine messages were often quite flattering for these students, and they normally involved some important task that only they themselves could fulfill. Prideful spiritual elitism is at odds with the responses to divine revelations found in Scripture, which, in spite of Joseph's dream about the sheaves (Genesis 37), sounded a lot more like "woe is me, for I am ruined!" (Isaiah 6:5 NAS) or "depart from me, for I am a sinful man" (Luke 5:8) or "I fell at his feet as though dead" (Revelation 1:17).

THE SPIRITUALITY OF NONEXPERIENCE

In spite of our emphasis on feeling and experiencing in Christian spirituality, those so-called "dry seasons" are actually biblical.[17] The nonexperience of divine abandonment is actually a dimension of the spiritual life found throughout Scripture:

> Behold, I go forward, but he is not there,
>   and backward, but I do not perceive him;

> on the left hand when he is working, I do not behold him;
>   he turns to the right hand, but I do not see him. (Job 23:8-9)

I am weary with my crying out;
  my throat is parched.
My eyes grow dim
  with waiting for my God. (Psalm 69:3)

Truly, you are a God who hides yourself,
  O God of Israel, the Savior. (Isaiah 45:15)

You have wrapped yourself with a cloud
  so that no prayer can pass through. (Lamentations 3:44)

Eloi, Eloi, lema sabachthani? (Mark 15:34)

To disparage someone because they do not feel or experience anything spiritually wondrous may amount to joining Job's friends in disparaging "a blameless and upright man" (Job 1:8) and to join the bystanders on Golgotha in disparaging One who "saved others" but seemed unable to "save himself" (Mark 15:31).

Seasons of nonexperience are inevitable. We need a spirituality mature enough to endure Mount Nebo and Golgotha as well as Mount Sinai and the Mount of the Transfiguration. Practicing the *gifts* of the Spirit is much easier than practicing the *fruits* of the Spirit—our assignment is often not so much to prophesy or speak in tongues but to practice "patience" and "faithfulness" (Galatians 5:22) when our quiet times are eerily too quiet. What takes more faith, to rejoice when the presence of God is palpable and clear, or to rejoice in the aching pain of divine absence? "In his economy of salvation, God needs faith which feels nothing, self-surrender which sees nothing, blind hope which seems to stretch out its hand into the void"—that's from Hans Urs von Balthasar.[18] In discussing contemplative prayer, he also writes that

> after the few months or years of initial enthusiasm, contemplation enters a stage of testing. Have we really based our lives on

the word of God, drawing sustenance from it as earthly men are sustained by earthly food? Do we really do [contemplative prayer] as a reverent service offered to divine love, and not out of a *spiritual egoism which is trying to enrich itself or amass spiritual pleasures?*[19]

The persistence of "dry times" tests our hearts to ensure our longings are ultimately for God himself rather than for comforting feelings or impressive experiences.

In spite of the inevitability of "dry times," we all long for a palpable sense of God. When my little daughter is afraid to fall asleep at night, I try to be helpful and suggest she ask Jesus to hold her: "After all, he is always with you no matter what, sweetie."

"But Daddy, I can't feel Jesus hugging me. I want *you* to stay and hug me."

She makes a very practical point. I suppose I could make the unrealistic and ultimately unhelpful promise to stay by her side at all times. This would not go very far in teaching her to trust in the superior power and omniscient presence of Jesus, but how do I explain that he is indeed at her side in spite the fact that he is physically intangible? How do I explain that Jesus would be much more handy than her dad should a storm arise or the bogeyman appear? I recently read her this passage from 1 Peter:

> Though you have not seen him, you love him. Though you do not now see him, you believe in him and rejoice with joy that is inexpressible and filled with glory, obtaining the outcome of your faith, the salvation of your souls. (1 Peter 1:8-9)[20]

The Lord we serve is mostly unfelt and unseen. But we *believe* in him, choosing to "walk by faith, not by sight" (2 Corinthians 5:7), and in that believing faith we can validly experience joy inexpressible. Again, when Thomas had his doubts removed by the physical presence of the resurrected Christ, he heard this with his own ears "blessed are those who have *not* seen and yet have believed" (John 20:29, emphasis added).

THE CYNICAL RESPONSES OF SKEPTICISM
AND HYPOSPIRITUALITY

From the previous sections it is hopefully clear that a certain degree of healthy skepticism must be brought to bear on feelings and mystical experiences. Not only does John instruct us to "test the spirits" (1 John 4:1), but Paul told the Corinthians that after prophetic speaking the congregation must "weigh what is said" (1 Corinthians 14:29). Skepticism can get unhealthy real fast, though.

When that Canadian brother was trying to push me backward in Kentucky, seeds of unhealthy skepticism took root. Within a few years those seeds had flourished to the point that I was cynical toward denominations and individual Christians who emphasized the supernatural work of the Holy Spirit. And when someone was overtly emotional in regard to their faith, I had to resist the reflexive temptation to roll my eyes.

This cynicism was sinful. There is just no other way to describe it. Paul gave the charismatic believers in Corinth certain means to assess supernatural manifestations. One of these means was the test of edification. Did the manifestation edify (that is, build up) the church? The verbal and noun form of the Greek word for *edifying* or *edification* is used seven times in 1 Corinthians 14. Those who view charismatics critically are quick to point out this litmus test of edification, but had this same test been applied to my former cynicism toward the supernatural and emotional, then I would have been in as much need of communal reproof as someone giving an uninterpreted message in tongues back in Corinth. My cynical skepticism was destructive, not edifying.

Paul's strongest corrective for the misuse of spiritual gifts is love. Though we primarily associate the "Love Chapter" (1 Corinthians 13) with wedding ceremonies, the original context is a church torn over the dysfunctional practices of spiritual gifts. Paul informs them that no matter how extraordinarily or sensationally the Spirit seems to be working, if there is no love, then speaking in tongues is just "a noisy gong or a clanging cymbal," and one who practices "prophetic powers" is "nothing" (1 Corinthians 13:1-2). Even an impassioned devotion to the extent of martyrdom gains "nothing" without love (v. 3).

Paul also writes, however, that love is not "arrogant," "rude," "irritable or resentful" (1 Corinthians 13:4-5), terms that often describe the demeanor of cynics toward experientialism.

Along with harboring a skeptical arrogance toward feelings and mystical experiences, Christian cynics begin practicing what I am calling "hypospirituality." If we talk too openly among cynical Christians about the sweet sense of Christ's love we experienced in our prayers that morning, or if we enthusiastically raise our hands in worship, then we might get that dreaded accusation mentioned in chapter 1 of being "hyperspiritual" (the prefixes *hyper* and *hypo* refer to "over" and "under," respectively). In cynical circles, being associated with hyperspirituality would be the height of insult! To fit in among cynical Christians, you would need to display antiemotional stances toward Christ and the gospel, poke fun at charismatic televangelists and occasionally toss out irreverent comments. Being unspiritual is actually more "spiritual" among Christian cynics for whom antiemotional hypospirituality is the (distorted) spirituality of choice.

Jonathan Edwards wrote his *Treatise Concerning Religious Affections* not just to critique emotional and spiritual abuses during the Great Awakening (1730s-1740s), but also to critique the skeptical reactions to the revival of many of his contemporaries throughout New England. The inappropriate responses to the authentic work of the Spirit during the Awakening pushed many to the extreme of suspicious cynicism.

> Because many who, in this late extraordinary season, appeared
> to have great religious affections, did not manifest a right tem-
> per of mind, and run [sic] into many errors, in the heat of their
> zeal; and because the high affections of many seem to be so
> soon come to nothing, and some who seemed to be mightily
> raised and swallowed with joy and zeal for a while, seemed to

have returned like a dog to his vomit: hence religious affections in general are grown out of credit with great numbers, as though true religion did not at all consist in them. Thus we easily and naturally run from one extreme to another.[21]

Though Edwards acknowledges the dangers and grievances of experientialism, he also chastens the shunning of emotional responses to God: "He who has no religious affection, is in a state of spiritual death." He condemns "heat without light," that is, fervor and passion devoid of knowledge or wisdom, but he also condemns "light without heat," which he describes as "a head stored with notions and speculations with a cold and unaffected heart."[22]

The extreme reaction of antiemotional and hypospiritual cynicism may be as much in error as sensational and hyperspiritual experientialism. We must not deemphasize the role of the Holy Spirit in our lives, without whom Paul tells us we cannot make the confession "Jesus is Lord" (1 Corinthians 12:3). Three times throughout 1 Corinthians 12–14 Paul instructs his readers to "earnestly desire" to be a vessel of the Spirit's supernatural activity within the congregation (1 Corinthians 12:31; 14:1, 39). We are told not to "quench the Spirit" (1 Thessalonians 5:19) but to "be filled with the Spirit" (Ephesians 5:18) or we will be named among the "scoffers . . . devoid of the Spirit" (Jude 18-19). And how can we emotionally disengage from a Lord who "rejoiced in the Holy Spirit" (Luke 10:21) and, in a violent display of emotion, "wept" at Lazarus's tomb? (John 11:35).

CORPUS CHRISTI DISMEMBERED?

The extremism Jonathan Edwards observed in his day certainly seems to feature in contemporary debates over emotions and mystical experiences. The church today is sharply polarized between those who embrace the sensationally supernatural and those who prefer to keep such "weird" stuff at arm's length.

Sadly, church demographics are frequently determined in our society by socioeconomic status and racial background. They are also determined to a certain degree by *spiritual-gift distribution*. This occurs when those of us who have one particular type of gift flock together. Though Paul envisioned the local congregation functioning as a body comprising multiple members with differing gifts (1 Corinthians 12; Romans 12:4-8; cf. Ephesians 4:1-16), we have now created situations where the more dramatic spiritual gifts are allowed to thrive without the corrective influence of those gifts that are perhaps a bit less glamorous. Disaffected intellectual teaching is regularly allowed to thrive without the balancing effects of more emotional personality types and dramatic displays of supernatural power. We have dismembered ourselves from a more diverse experience of body life and conglomerated with similar dismembered parts, thereby eliminating the intended tension provided by complementary and mutually corrective gifts. Does our local church function as a body or as a collection of fingers or ears? In this homogenous set up, all the hands have gathered on one street corner with the legs across the street and the eyes a few blocks down.

The solution to the current dismembered status of the church requires something terribly awkward: emotional enthusiasts and cynical skeptics need to hang out over coffee and start worshiping together.

One of my greatest challenges in campus ministry was providing one worship service for a diverse population of university students. The Christian university I served at the time was not quite large enough to sustain multiple campus ministries. In spite of the school's size, the backgrounds and dispositions of these students were quite varied. Cynical religious studies majors, who loved studying the Bible in Greek, were alongside conservative legalists, who were trying to extend their youth group experience into college life. There were artsy students who didn't care if they fit in with anyone, as well as an extremely vocal charismatic faction that regularly visited the "prophecy booths" at a nearby Pentecostal megachurch.

Only one worship service was available.

The religious studies students wanted carefully crafted theological sermons that made irreverent jabs at youth-group spirituality. The youth group kids wanted to have more fun activities. The art students wanted poetics. The charismatics just wanted to get "krunked for Jesus" and witness to the lost. The task for our campus ministry leadership team in ministering to all of them through one service was daunting.

Something feels a little weird in saying this, but I have found that much of my ministerial experience has been occupied with playing "devil's advocate." After four years of meticulous relational work (gentle nudges, hard confrontations, uncomfortable meetings, etc.), we began to see the relational lines drawn between those opposing camps become more and more permeable. We started doing double takes on campus, noticing a charismatic student hanging out with an intellectual philosophy student, an art student laughing with a traditional Baptist student. Four years of that awkward relational work was finally found to be worthwhile.

If you are cynical toward emotions and the supernatural, invite some folks who regularly see visions and pray for worldwide revival to join you for coffee. You'll be good for each other.

CONCLUDING STORY: A FEELING, AN EXPERIENCE AND THIS BOOK

In chapter two I recounted how I became disillusioned after returning from my round-the-world journey and visiting the campus ministry in which I had invested so much during college. What so disturbed me was that I found it unhealthily abuzz with the sensational and the supernatural. Those seeds of doubt toward charismatic experiences and feelings had been sown previously, especially in the scene where I found myself on the receiving end of a push to the forehead that was supposed to send me to the floor "slain in the Spirit."

I want to close on a different note.

Though feelings should be processed with a hearty dose of distrust, I have long sensed the impulse to write. This feeling has intensified over the past several years as I began developing the material for this book. I remember sheepishly peddling sample chapters to editors amid the bookstalls at a handful of Society of Biblical Literature meetings. No one accepted my work, but the feeling that I should and must write persisted.

While writing furiously with no viable hope whatsoever of an interested publisher, I attended a reunion for folks who used to be involved in that campus ministry back at the University of Georgia. Though my cynicism toward charismatic expressions of Christian faith had largely dissipated, I was a bit intimidated when my wife and I were placed in the midst of my fellow alumni for the purpose of prayer and "prophecy." Though none of them knew of my aspirations to write, someone cited from Psalm 45:1 during the prayer time—"my tongue is like the pen of a ready scribe"—and then asked that God would grant me a ministry in writing. After the time of prayer, my former campus minister wanted to know if I had ever considered writing, because while praying, God had told him, "You are going to read a book that Andy is going to write." None of them knew that I had been so passionately working on this book project.

Eventually, a publisher (graciously) accepted my submission. So let me close this chapter on experientialism affirming that I believe that God works experientially in our lives. Sometimes feelings are neurological phenomena unrelated to spirituality; but sometimes they are the manifestations of divine impulses mysteriously placed within us. Sometimes supernatural experiences are sourced in the wiles of complex spiritual powers that are unrelated to the activity of the Holy Spirit; but sometimes the Spirit blatantly ignores the normal way of things and does something extramundane and dramatic. We are charged with being responsible with our emotions and wise with our experiences, but not to the extent that we reject all feelings and quench the work of the third person of the Trinity.

DISCUSSION QUESTIONS

1. Have experiences and emotions played a large or a small role in your spiritual history? What role do they play today?

2. Have the times when God was deeply teaching and molding you

been accompanied by emotional "warm fuzzies" or by something else? If something else, describe.

3. Have you ever made a decision based on your emotions or dramatic experiences, and then later realized that you were misguided by those emotions? Explain.

4. Have you ever seen or experienced something supernatural, but it didn't seem to be from God? Describe.

5. When you think of the "most devoted followers of Christ" that you know, what attributes cause you to consider them as such? Is there anyone not characteristically emotional who you consider to be extremely devoted to Christ?

6   # anti-intellectualism

*The scandal of the evangelical mind
is that there is not much of an
evangelical mind. . . . American
evangelicals are not exemplary for their
thinking, and they have not been so for several
generations.*

—Mark Noll, *The Scandal of the Evangelical Mind*

*Brothers, do not be children in your thinking. Be infants in evil, but in
your thinking be mature.*

1 Corinthians 14:20

*When you come, bring the cloak that I left with Carpus at Troas, also
the books, and above all the parchments.*

2 Timothy 4:13

Late in the spring they are invited to stand in the worship services
before proud, approving faces. Their names are affectionately read
aloud, and in response they proceed to the pulpit to receive a brand

new Bible and perhaps some sentimental trinket purchased in the "Gifts for Graduates" section of the local Christian bookstore. Parents and former Sunday school teachers beam as the high school seniors descend from the podium and resume their seats. The minister offers a moving prayer on their behalf, asking God to change the world into which the church now sends them. After the worship service there is a group photo and possibly a fine lunch on the grounds.

Four months later, with leaves beginning to fall on the quad surrounding the religious studies department, some of these students will be asked questions about their crisp new Bibles, and they will have no satisfactory answers. Why does Matthew have Jesus riding two donkeys for the "triumphal entry" and Mark only has him riding one? Why are there so few shared miracles and Jesus-sayings between John and the other Gospels? Why does Paul say Abraham was not "justified by works" (Romans 4:2) whereas James asks rhetorically, "was not our father Abraham justified by works" (James 2:21)? Why would you assume Moses wrote the Pentateuch when his own death is recorded in Deuteronomy? How can you serve a God who commanded genocide during the conquest of Canaan? How can you assert the historicity of Acts when Luke's account of Paul's life differs from Paul's own account in Galatians? Which way did Judas die, by hanging as Matthew describes or by taking a spill while running as described by Luke?

To these questions, most of our proud high school graduates, many of them with more than a decade of Sunday school training under their belts, will simply have to say, "I don't know. I just don't know." Some of them will clutch their new Bibles all the more tightly, sparring with their "liberal" professors in class or perhaps rapidly withdrawing from the religion course in protest (and in fear).

Others will leave those crisp, new Bibles crisp and new from disillusioned disuse.

JUDAS TWICE DEAD
Relieved that we have somehow kept adolescents in our pews long

enough to see them graduate high school, we then send some of them off to university campuses where their faith can so easily crash, burn and fade away at the pedagogical jabs of a religious studies professor. A collision with biblical criticism can expose the naivety nurtured under the shelter of their churches, and both Scripture and theological traditions may well end up as flotsam and jetsam, hastily discarded as unnecessary trappings on the stormy waters of early adulthood. Varied versions of the scenario described in the previous section are quite common, and not just for secular universities—I have witnessed this violent bursting of bubbles on Christian campuses as much as I saw it as an undergraduate at a large state school.

About the time I was supposed to declare my major while attending that large state school, I embraced a call to ministry that required an overhaul of former plans. There was so much I could learn in the university context to prepare me in this new vocational path—Greek, Hebrew, church history, theology, Greco-Roman culture, biblical studies and the like. But the religion department at the University of Georgia had gained notoriety among many of my Christian friends as being hostile to Christianity. I was attending a New Testament introduction course at the time, which turned up stones I would have preferred to have kept unturned.

So I became a forestry major.

Yes, forestry. I grew up around the woods and I liked being outdoors. But more to the point, I did not want my faith to be ripped to shreds by the religion professors. I ended up taking a few electives in religious studies, but for the most part I was spending my classroom time learning about dendrology and forest ecology instead of Old Testament and second temple Judaism.

Rather than studiously working on my forestry degree, however, I spent time out of class devouring my Bible, and with very little guidance beyond my peers. Though I was spared from tests on the JEDP theory (a controversial explanation of the Old Testament's formation) during my undergraduate days, I began to notice disturbing phenomena in the pages of my Bible. There was the temptation to avoid the occasional discrepancies or the slight theological inconsistencies I seemed to be finding, or at least to suspend my intellectual wrangling over those troublesome issues until I made it to seminary (where, presumably, everything fuzzy would be made crystal clear). But the anti-intellectual avoidance of my own hard questions began to seem as dishonorable to Scripture as having those questions in the first place. So one day I asked a Christian scholar I knew about the two accounts of Judas's death (Matthew 27:3-10; Acts 1:18-19). I braced myself for an upbraiding—I knew my query could be perceived as a threatening act of rebellion. As it turns out, he did not respond with authoritative annoyance. He provided me with the explanation that had been given him at some point when he had once daringly ventured the same question:

> Since Matthew tells us Judas hanged himself and since Luke tells us that Judas died by falling [and then bursting into a messy pile of human carnage], and since Scripture is the Word of God and therefore, as Jesus said, "cannot be broken" (John 10:35), then clearly the rope Judas used *broke*, and when the rope snapped he began running in the field to which Luke refers before falling to his death.

At first I marveled at the creativity of the explanation and experienced a bit of relief that an explanation was even possible.

The relief was short-lived.

The interpretive acrobatics at work in the explanation were motivated by a desire to honor Scripture, but the melding together of the two accounts seemed to dishonor the separate canonical voices of both Matthew and Luke. My scholarly friend had shared the explanation with veiled dissatisfaction himself. The alternative of affirming two distinct (yet conflicting) accounts seemed an act of rebellion against his church tradition.

Then again, conflating two distinct accounts into one seemed like an act of rebellion against the canonical witness of Scripture.

If someone reads her Bible enough to come up with a question like,

"Why are there different accounts of the same event?" it is unlikely
that she will feel comfortable posing that question in her Sunday
school class. The church is for solid, clear answers, not pesky, curious
questions, right? Due to this common defensive resistance to addressing hard questions that demand careful intellectual inquiry, the quer-
ulous Bible reader is often forced to look for resources *outside the
realm* of the church. The questions may get tabled silently out of reverence temporarily, but eventually the pressure of internal intellectual
tumult grows unmanageable. At this point, all it takes to destabilize
the faith of the troubled Bible reader is glancing over the back cover of
a Bart Ehrman book at Barnes & Noble or bumping into that atheist
friend who checked out of youth group years earlier when he faced the
same questions.

So when our high school seniors triumphantly graduate in May
and then find their faith rattled at the university in the fall, where
does the fault most lie—with the intellectual elitism of the academy
that asks too many questions or with the anti-intellectualism of the
church that permits too few? The belligerence of the occasional religious studies professor who prods and stabs may be less at fault than
the negligence of the church that is failing to train and teach.

In a landmark sociological study of the religious life of American
teenagers, Christian Smith and Melinda Lundquist Denton concluded
that "religious education in the United States is currently failing with
youth when it comes to the articulation of faith."[1] Christians may spend
their entire childhood and adolescence in the church and never receive
adequate training about their faith traditions or about the complexities
and complications of biblical and theological issues. Without this nurture and training, the faith of our young adults will likely become a
tertiary concern in their lives, especially when what little instruction
they *have* received is exposed as oversimplified and underdeveloped.

AN UNFORTUNATE CYCLE

When I began making plans to attend seminary, I was encouraged by
some and chastised by others. Among the latter were some elders who

clearly viewed the academic instruction of theology and biblical studies with suspicious contempt. Others were chary with their approval, issuing the warning that I make certain to maintain a separate devotional life outside the classroom assignments, presumably because those academic assignments would be disconnected from the health of my soul. Then I entered seminary and kept wondering why I had never heard any of this material before. *Why had no one ever pointed out those brilliant instances of literary intercalation in Mark? Why had I never heard about Athanasius? Why had I never recited the Nicene Creed? How could I have attended church for two decades and never learned about the Babylonian exile?* When my Old Testament professor at Beeson Divinity School told me to read the book of Job one night for homework, I wondered how such an assignment could be viewed as dangerously disjointed from the regular Bible readings of my "quiet times."

Years earlier when I attended New Testament intro at UGA, I was thrilled to have with me a dear Christian friend who happened to be one of the smartest guys I knew. Of the openly Christian minority in the classroom, he alone could heroically stand up to the ostensibly scandalous propositions of the professor. Unlike me (the guy who declared forestry as his major that same semester), he chose to remain on north campus and keep slogging away in the religious studies courses. Before long, he was being affirmed by his Christian peers to pursue an academic path in order that he might be a light in the dark realm of academia. But when he began wrestling with the intellectual complexities that attend any serious study of the Bible, some of his friends looked askance at his newly acquired learning and wondered if he was slipping off those slippery slopes and permitting intellectualism to compromise his faith.

Grasped by the beautiful intricacies of the Bible, intrigued by the arduous work of theologians in centuries past, mesmerized by extinct languages scribbled on ostraca or crumbling vellum pages, so many young Christians eagerly embark on a life of biblical scholarship only to discover that the church they are deeply devoted to is either disinterested in their rigorous intellectual labors or even downright disapproving of their research. Many Christians have been historically inhospitable to their brothers and sisters serving Christ in the academic context. Such an unwelcome disposition understandably disillusions large numbers of these Christian intellectuals who have endured countless late nights and painfully paid thousands in tuition fees while suffering through multiple degree programs, all for the sake of a thankless church that esteems their work as meaningless at best or pernicious at worst.

When the apostle Paul described the church as a "body," he warned against certain members of the community declaring to other members "I have no need of you" (1 Corinthians 12:21), yet in American religious history, this has been the message received by many of the church's brightest and most studious members. Such inhospitality can easily leave Christian scholars so embittered and jaded that they begin taking sick delight in bursting the bubbles of the idealistic students fresh out of youth group, many of whom enter those courses in the first place because they want training for ministerial service. As the church's negligence to nurture the life of the mind continues, so also continues the belligerent gouging and prodding of cynical religious studies professors. The cycle seems self-perpetuating.

As for my intellectual friend, however, I am pleased to report that after three academic degrees from some of the most impressive institutions in the world, he now teaches New Testament intro courses at a state school, similar to the course we both sat in over fifteen years ago. Now *he* is the one daily addressing the protests and fearful queries signaled by the raised hands of the vocal Christian minorities in the back of his classroom. He loves biblical scholarship. He also loves Jesus.

INTELLECTUAL ESCAPISM IN THE CHURCH: "THE BIBLE SAYS IT, THAT SETTLES IT"

So where does this Christian anti-intellectualism come from? Whence all the reluctance in embracing the value of intellectual labors on behalf of Christ's kingdom? There are a number of studies that trace the development of anti-intellectualism in the evangelical church.[2] I will attempt to provide here a cursory (and admittedly oversimplified) summary.

A good place to start is with Jonathan Edwards, perhaps the greatest mind in America's evangelical heritage. Though there is a renewed interest in Edwards today, it is curious that the Puritan pastor, theologian and philosopher seems to have had no comparable "intellectual successors" in the generations of evangelicals that followed him.[3]

As we noticed in the chapter on experientialism, Edwards supported the Great Awakening that took place in the 1730s and 1740s. In spite of this support he was meticulously careful not to promote an imbalanced emphasis on feelings and spiritual experiences (which he collectively called "affections") that would sabotage the equally valid work of the mind. It seems that Edwards's cautious embrace of that great revival inadvertently contributed to what historians call "revivalism," an approach to ministry that emphasizes emotional responses, which can be effectively engineered through certain techniques and skills.[4] In a noble attempt to bring the gospel message into frontier and rural America, itinerant preachers understandably avoided technical theological lingo to appeal to common folks who lacked the educational backgrounds of those back on the seaboard. Eventually, however, this absence of traditional theological language and the appeal to the emotions over the mind naturally contributed to anti-intellectualism among early Americans. (Edwards would have been quite displeased!) This revivalism also featured the exaltation of those passionate itinerant preachers to celebrity status. Authority began shifting from theologically trained ministers to energetic preachers whose charismatic personalities commanded allegiance: "The pastor was no longer a teacher who instructs a covenanted congregation, but a celebrity who is able to inspire mass audiences."[5]

As a nation that had just successfully cast off the fetters of the British Crown, the Revolutionary-era disgust with authority helped fuel the populist distrust of trained clergy.[6] The American religious traditions had strong historical ties with denominations and movements back in Europe, so "disestablishment" became the order of the day (a.k.a., separation of church and state).[7] The growing American individualism balked at institutional authority that smacked of the tyranny exerted by European kings, bishops and the pope. This was the New World, and with the Declaration of Independence, American Christians believed they were entering a new *ecclesiastical* epoch as much as a new *political* epoch—the centuries of Christianity's captivity to a corrupt church could now be cast aside to make way for a return to the (presumably) untarnished New Testament church. There was a certain degree of legitimacy to these new ideas in those early evangelical circles, but dangers abounded.

> The cavalier rejection of the past stripped the church of the rich resources of centuries' worth of theological reflection, Scriptural meditation, and spiritual experience. It inculcated an attitude that there was nothing to be gained from grappling with the thought of the great minds of the past—Augustine and Tertullian, Bernard of Clairvaux and Thomas Aquinas, Martin Luther and John Calvin. It was an approach doomed, almost by definition, to anti-intellectualism and theological shallowness.[8]

So even before the Civil War, evangelical life in America was characterized by an uncritical blending of religious ideas with patriotism, an exaltation of magnetic pastors and preachers, and a neglect of historical theology (that is, the creeds and theological wisdom of centuries past).

Does any of this ring familiar with contemporary church life in America? Patriotism: I went to my local Christian bookstore recently and the most prominent display was for *The Patriot Bible*. Celebrity ministers: I just visited the website of a megachurch in my city and noticed that "Meet Our Pastor" seemed to be one of the main themes. Historical and theological illiteracy: Ever heard the slogan "No Creed but the Bible"? Sometimes it is announced with the gusto of a baptismal oath.

The antihistorical and antiauthoritarian disposition of young America's populist Christians was also influenced by Enlightenment ideologies that were thick in the cultural air of the time. Various elements of this new way of thinking were taken as axiomatic and contributed in rather bizarre and unsuspecting ways to the fundamentalism of the latter nineteenth century and early twentieth centuries. This conservative movement scrambled to hold Christian ground when the secular intelligentsia began promoting models of scientific inquiry that challenged the older models that had been adopted by evangelical believers.[9] The divide between intellectuals and populist Christianity thus was expanded. In a positive sense conservative Christians energetically gave themselves to mass evangelism, overseas missions and social justice work. Negatively, these endeavors were undertaken outside of a biblically shaped intellectual framework, thereby promoting what Martin Marty has called "the idolization of the 'doer' as opposed to the 'thinker.'"[10]

Once upon a time in American Christianity, anti-intellectualism was understood as a rejection of the established church. The protests were so successful in the evangelical tradition that today the situation is reversed—*intellectualism* is now often understood as a rejection of the established church.

INSIGHT WITHOUT LOVE: THE CYNICISM OF THE INTELLECTUALLY BETRAYED

So how does the powerful heritage of anti-intellectualism impact the Christian who has an insatiable appetite for studying and learning more about God, the Bible and the theological traditions of the church? Sadly, the potential for becoming a cynical intellectual is enormous.

Some of the most cynical Christians I have met are religious studies majors and seminary students from conservative backgrounds. Having bravely endured the initial shocks that Paul may not have written Ephesians and that Martin Luther unabashedly enjoyed beer, these young believers must then commence to process knowledge they never learned after countless Vacation Bible Schools and years of Sunday school. Their intellectual wrestling is frequently under the guidance of a few cynical professors who enjoy disabusing the naive. While learning about textual criticism in biblical studies courses and reading about undignified theological debates in church history class, these students gain a wide range of new—and at times disillusioning—insights.

When children mature and begin discovering family secrets, they often develop of sense of betrayal: *Why didn't my parents tell me about this?* Similarly, when young students of theology and biblical studies begin sifting through library shelves and discover skeletons shoved into the church's closet, they wonder, *Why didn't my pastor tell me about this?* The students also begin quaking in awed delight over the wonders they find in reading dead theologians. They find themselves trembling over the profound beauty of God's Word. But then they wonder, as I did, *Why was it necessary to enroll in a college or divinity school to hear about this?* Gaining both inspiring and disillusioning insights to which the church seems so flippant can leave these Christian students with the sense that they have been intellectually betrayed. The ensuing distrust sometimes leads them into cynicism, and there are many jaded intellectuals out there willing to guide these Christians way down into the dark (or what they may deem as the light).

The experience of disillusionment within the religious studies classroom has become, for many Christians, an initiatory rite of sorts into the ranks of the intellectual elite. Within these ranks skepticism is celebrated as a defining characteristic of the new spirituality of the jaded much the way passion and enthusiasm are celebrated as defining marks of spirituality in more charismatic circles.

The disturbing irony is that many of these young cynics will become the future ministers of the church. They entered seminaries and religious studies programs with the earnest desire to serve local congregations. By the time they have finished their degree, however, many of these students will find themselves eager to burst a few bubbles on their own, contemptuously eyeing the unenlightened masses within the church. Many unsuspecting laypersons will unwittingly become targets of the young minister's intellectual frustrations. As noted throughout this book, the Christian subculture certainly embraces much incorrect teaching without cautious critique (hence, "pop Christianity"), but the chief motivation for those offering correction often is not so much a love for truth but a desire to demonstrate intellectual superiority. In my own academic studies I have found at times the propensity to demonstrate *insight* without demonstrating *love*. This intellectual cynicism can be described as an awakened awareness to truth unperceived by others, coupled with a lack of love for those failing to perceive it.

In the church, intellectual cynicism is certainly not limited to seminarians and nineteen-year-olds in undergraduate religious studies courses. And many seminarians and religious studies majors are *not* cynical—many professors I know who teach those courses are *not* among the embittered intelligentsia who harbor a grudge against the church. But the ongoing cycle generated by anti-intellectualism in the church and intellectual elitism in the academy may be among the most serious issues Christians must address in our day.

Though the author of Ecclesiastes remarks that "the writing of many books is endless, and excessive devotion to books is wearying to the body" (Ecclesiastes 12:12 NASB), I have a book recommendation for young theological and biblical studies students. Helmut Thielicke's *A Little Exercise for Young Theologians* is indispensable because of its judicious warnings against the dangers of gaining a big head while commencing advanced theological studies. (I should also point out that the book is pleasantly short!) This German professor had seen the damaging effects of intellectual superiority after years of instructing bright young enthusiasts in the fields of theology and biblical studies.

He contends that the spiritual maturity of novice theologians is often less developed than their head knowledge: "There is a hiatus between the area of the young theologian's actual spiritual growth and what he already knows intellectually about this arena."[11] He goes on to write that young theologians manifest certain trumped-up intellectual effects that actually amount to nothing.

Speaking figuratively, the study of theology often produces overgrown youths whose internal organs have not correspondingly developed. This is a characteristic of adolescence. There is actually something like *theological* puberty.[12]

Thielicke urges young Christian scholars to ensure that their intellectual training never exceeds their spiritual maturity (or to at least be aware of the potential gap between the two). Ministers fresh out of divinity school who pridefully disparage their congregations for a lack of theological knowledge will only reinforce the anti-intellectualism they are so annoyed with. The pastor must be gentle and patient as a teacher (just as the congregation will have to be a gentle and patient teacher of the pastor). Again, from Thielicke:

In his reflective detachment the theologian feels himself superior to those who, in their personal relationship to Christ, completely pass over the problems of the historical Jesus or demythologizing or the objectivity of salvation.

This disdain is a *spiritual disease*. It lies in the conflict between truth and love. This conflict is precisely *the* disease of theologians.[13]

THE LIFE OF THE MIND: BIBLICAL MANDATES AND WARNINGS

Someone asked Jesus which commandment from the law was most important.

Jesus answered,

The most important is, "Hear, O Israel: The Lord our God, the Lord is one. And you shall love the Lord your God with all your heart and with all your soul *and with all your mind* and with all your strength." The second is this: "You shall love your neighbor as yourself." There is no other commandment greater than these. (Mark 12:29-31, emphasis added)

Jesus cites not from the Ten Commandments, but from the passage introduced by the *Shema* (from the Hebrew verb "to hear"): "Hear, O

Israel: The LORD our God, the LORD is one" (Deuteronomy 6:4). Immediately following this command (which has been recited daily by devout Jews since before Jesus' day) is the command to love God with all of our being, including our *minds*.[14] Jesus then appends to this Leviticus 19:18, demonstrating that a love for God is never to be disconnected from a love of people.

Most Christians could readily answer the Sunday school question, What is the greatest commandment? But we rarely think about the *context* of the *Shema*. In the wider passage (the co-text, if you will), loving God with our entire being is inseparable from knowing and meditating on his *words:*

> Hear, O Israel: The LORD our God, the LORD is one. You shall love the LORD your God with all your heart and with all your soul and with all your might. *And these words* that I command you today shall be on your heart. You shall teach them diligently to your children, and shall talk of them when you sit in your house, and when you walk by the way, and when you lie down, and when you rise. You shall bind them as a sign on your hand, and they shall be as frontlets between your eyes. You shall write them on the doorposts of your house and on your gates. (Deuteronomy 6:4-9, emphasis added)

Here we see that the context of the highest demand placed on our lives as Christians—loving God with everything—is the diligent instruction and unending discussion of Scripture. There is no arena of our lives—"when you sit in your house, and when you walk by the way, and when you lie down, and when you rise"—that can be divorced from a constant engagement with God's words. We should not have to go to seminary to become a serious student of Scripture: the words of God are to be unavoidably present in all aspects of a believer's life (figuratively speaking, on our hands, between our eyes, in our houses and on our gates).

The neglect of serious, mature thinking stands in direct conflict with that which is most binding in our lives: the greatest commandment according to Jesus.

Nonetheless, severe warnings are necessary. In claiming to honor the first commandment of loving God with everything, including our minds, intellectual Christians may break the *second* commandment by failing to love those neighbors who may not care about the latest title from the Society of Biblical Literature or the latest debate at the American Academy of Religion. There is a problem when those who can read the Bible in Greek suddenly feel more important than the linguistically limited masses. There is a problem when someone gets snubbed or laughed at because he or she has never heard of Karl Barth or Albert Schweitzer. There is a problem when we feel spiritually superior because we read Miroslav Volf instead of the trendy bestsellers displayed in the Christian book section at Walmart.

Gaining insight tends to inflate our egos. Paul saw this at work among the Corinthian believers who boasted in impressive spiritual knowledge: "This 'knowledge' puffs up, but love builds up" (1 Corinthians 8:1). In 1 Corinthians 13:2 Paul writes that if I "understand all mysteries and all knowledge, . . . *but have not love*, I am nothing" (emphasis added)—insight without love is condemned.

Nothing illustrates the dangers of intellectualism and impressive erudition than the scene in Eden's garden beside that lovely tree. Lust for special illumination and esoteric knowledge got humanity all messed up in the first place:

> The serpent said to the woman, "You will not surely die. For God knows that when you eat of it your eyes will be opened, and you will be like God, knowing good and evil." So when the woman saw that the tree was good for food, and that it was a delight to the eyes, and that the tree was to be desired to make one wise [or "to give insight"], she took of its fruit and ate, and she also gave some to her husband who was with her, and he ate. (Genesis 3:4-6)

The haunting account of the Fall demonstrates that the pursuit of knowledge for the sake of knowledge is potentially devastating. The *knowing* we must be devoted to is ultimately knowing a Person, God.

Since he is most imminently presented to us in his carefully crafted written Word, then we must devote ourselves to mature thinking. But those with mature thinking do not gloat over God's Word. They *tremble*.

> This is the one to whom I will look:
> he who is humble and contrite in spirit
> and trembles at my word. (Isaiah 66:2)

DISCUSSION QUESTIONS

1. What has been one of the most shocking discoveries you have made about the Bible that you never learned growing up?

2. When you have come across difficult bits of Scripture or theology, how have you responded? Has it caused you to delve deeper into the quest for truth or to throw up your hands and give up?

3. Why do you think many Christians and churches dismiss the need for greater theological education?

4. In what setting have you been most encouraged to further your theological studies?

7   cultural irrelevance

The best vitamin for a Christian is B1.

—church marquee

Sometimes I think nothing better illustrates the beauty of Christ's intergenerational following than the wisdom discovered when a young person's ideas about the church collide with the ideas of our parents' or grandparents' generation.

—Sarah Cunningham, *Dear Church: Letters from a Disillusioned Generation*

To the Jews I became as a Jew. . . . To those under the law I became as one under the law. . . . To those outside the law I became as one outside the law. . . . To the weak I became weak. . . . I have become all things to all people that by all means I may save some.

1 Corinthians 9:20-22

If we really hope for the kingdom of God, then we can also endure the Church in its pettiness.

—Karl Barth, *Dogmatics in Outline*

After four years of campus ministry work, I began pastoring a small, traditional church on the outskirts of Durham, North Carolina. The sound of drums and acoustic guitars gave way to the sounds of an organ interspersed with the occasional hiss of a dear parishioner's oxygen tank. The aroma of brewing coffee was replaced with the fragrance of floral arrangements complemented by the floral hints of the perfume worn by great aunts and grandmothers. Reasons for missing Sunday morning services changed from sleeping in late to arthritis pain. Reasons for missing evening Bible studies changed from watching *Lost* or *American Idol* to the trepidation of driving at night once the daylight began disappearing earlier than usual in autumn.

In anticipation of my first visit to this church during the interview process, I wondered if they knew "Beulah Land," an old hymn I used to hear at my grandparents' little church out in the country. My wife and I entered the sanctuary at 11 a.m. on the nose that day, only to find that we were five minutes late—in keeping with the punctuality of "the greatest generation," the service had started early. After the "meet and greet" time when we shook welcoming hands there was a "special music" piece: "Beulah Land." Within a few weeks I began working as their interim pastor while I commenced studies nearby at Duke Divinity School.

An old plywood sign at the corner of U.S. Highway 70 and Old NC 10 pointed passersby our way. The words, painted long ago in an imitation Old English font, simply read—Mount Hermon Baptist Church, Est. 1848. Beneath the words there was an arrow conveying to prospective visitors that we were westward on Old NC 10. The sign's outdated font and aged disrepair may have inadvertently conveyed something else: *old, out-of-touch church.*

We didn't get many visitors.

GHETTO CHURCHIANITY

That sign on the corner of Old NC 10 and U.S. 70 could be seen as emblematic of one of the sharpest criticisms lodged against the church by its younger members: *cultural irrelevance.*

David Kinnaman and Gabe Lyons have researched Christianity's reputation among younger generations and published commentary on the findings in *unChristian: What a New Generation Really Thinks About Christianity . . . and Why It Matters.* An overwhelming number of that youthful demographic so glaringly absent from Sunday morning pews deem the church in America to be bigoted, hypocritical and sheltered, with little of consequence to offer them. For the purpose of this chapter, I am most concerned with the accusation of "sheltered."[1]

The church often expects young people to adjust their style and preferences: "We want young generations to participate in our churches, but we expect them to play by the rules, look the part, embrace the music, and use the right language."[2] This attitude repulses teens and young adults, who can find plenty of other ways to spend their time on Sunday mornings (like sleeping, if nothing else comes to mind). Honestly, what does a traditional little church that doesn't even have a PowerPoint projector have to offer twenty-somethings with iPhones? What do people who can hardly remember their first decade of marriage have to offer to a nineteen-year-old looking for a date? How could a choir and hand-bell ensemble appeal to a thirty-year-old who just bought Coldplay tickets? Steeped in a me-centered, media-saturated culture, many young people would view the offerings from a local congregation as irrelevant.

One of my first weekends in the Mount Hermon parsonage was spent collecting our postmove debris and stuffing it in trash bags. Since we didn't have a garbage pickup service, we had to take all of our trash around to the far side of the fellowship hall and toss it in the church dumpster.

Dressed in my rough, work-around-the-house clothes, I pulled my worn and slightly battered pickup truck next to that dumpster and started tossing in the trash. An urgent voice began shouting in the distance. I looked up to see one of the ladies in our congregation rushing my way from the side entrance of the church.

"*That is our dumpster!* No trash goes in that dumpster but what

comes from our church! That's not for public use! You have to go . . .
Oh . . . (ahem) . . . *Pastor—it's you.*" With the (rather embarrassing)
instance of recognition came an immediate shift in tone. I was just
standing there frozen, like a deer caught in headlights, a trash bag
clutched in hand.

Now, this is a dear lady who became a friend of mine, but at that
moment I realized just how much lay ahead of Mount Hermon in becoming more welcoming to our local community. If we yell at (apparent) strangers for using our dumpster, then I am not sure how welcome
unchurched neighbors would feel joining us for worship (if a church
can't handle other folks' trash, then what are we good for anyway?).

Several young people did actually meet on our grounds on a regular basis. They did not come to youth group or to a young couples Bible study—they came to shoot hoops in our parking lot. I learned that
some years back a former pastor had rigged up metal contraptions
and attached them to the basketball goals to keep the pesky kids away.
Thankfully these had been removed, so in spite of the dumpster inci-
dent, I knew that even though we had a long way to go, Mount Hermon had already been making some strides in becoming more welcoming to outsiders.

One of my favorite teachers on the church's struggles to engage our
rapidly changing society is Matt Orth, ministry director for Crossroads Worldwide and the teaching pastor of a young church in a rural
North Carolina community. I have heard him use this great word to
describe the insular church life that is confined to the provincial
"ghetto" of Christian subculture: *churchianity.*[3] Many of us tend to
treat our churches as safe enclaves for escapism rather than as launching pads for missional living. This churchianity promotes an institutional identity of the church and, while doing so, makes relevantly
engaging outsiders a tertiary concern. If a church does decide it must
reach outsiders, the motivation often comes from nothing more than
a feverish survival instinct to secure enough numbers to keep the institution alive.

Churchianity would not sit well with the apostle Paul. Not only did he strive to "become all things to all people" (1 Corinthians 9:22), he also persistently taught the early churches to be conscientious about their behavior toward "outsiders":

> If, therefore, the whole church comes together and all speak in tongues, and outsiders or unbelievers enter, will they not say that you are out of your minds? (1 Corinthians 14:23)

> Conduct yourselves wisely toward outsiders, making the best use of the time. (Colossians 4:5 ESV)

> Aspire to live quietly, and to mind your own affairs, and to work with your hands, as we instructed you, so that you may live properly before outsiders and be dependent on no one. (1 Thessalonians 4:11-12)

> Moreover, he [an authoritative church leader] must be well thought of by outsiders, so that he may not fall into disgrace, into a snare of the devil. (1 Timothy 3:7)

When Paul preached in Athens, he cited a Greek poet and used one of their own religious monuments for an illustration. When he visited the Jerusalem temple, he shaved his head as one committed to a Jewish religious vow. In his letters he provided careful instructions for Jewish Christians not to impose their own religious culture on Gentile Christians.

Churchianity doesn't sit well with Jesus, either. Nothing evidences the need for the gospel to be communicated crossculturally more than the incarnation, when the preexistent Son of God left his heavenly realm to enter the day-to-day grind of first-century Palestine. When "the Word became flesh" (John 1:14), God was going to the extreme to reach people in accessible, relevant ways.

So how is the church doing in serving One who inserted himself into the daily routines and struggles of an ancient culture in order to communicate his love? Many younger adults would answer *Not very well at all.*

THE CYNICAL RESPONSE OF CULTURAL ARROGANCE

It is hard not to be cynical when you drive past a church and read a message like this on a rusted marquee sign: To Prevent Sinburn, Use Sonscreen.

Really? Someone thought it was a good idea to go public with that? Someone please tell me we can be more creative in relating our theological convictions to the world than: "God Answers Kneemail."[4]

A few months ago my wife and I saw another church sign that made me cringe. It wasn't a marquee with plastic block letters, and it bore a much hipper font than Old English. It was not posted by a rural road out in the country. It was plastered across an enormous billboard high above an interstate outside Atlanta: Not Your Aunt Gertrude's Church.

Clearly, this ad was not sponsored by a traditional congregation but by a young, suburban church hoping to catch the interest of those disillusioned with Christianity's supposed irrelevance.

It offended me.

I agree with the accusation that many churches are culturally irrelevant. As a college pastor I most certainly mourn Christianity's widespread failure in connecting with young people. But after serving a church where Aunt Gertrude would have felt right at home, I wanted that north Atlanta billboard torn to the ground.

I spent two years with the folks at Mount Hermon Baptist Church. We made plans for a new sign off Old NC 10 and experimented with ideas for making the church more relevant to those moving into our surrounding community. I don't have a spectacular story about all the young people we began reaching with cultural relevance initiatives. I wished we had somehow reached them, not just because we needed them but because I had worked with younger people long enough to know that they needed the older community at Mount Hermon.

I finished my degree at Duke and eventually left this little congregation to lead a vibrant college ministry based out of a suburban church in Birmingham, Alabama. Announcing my plans to leave Mount Hermon was one of the most painful moments in my ministerial experience. I wept and coughed and blew my nose all over the pulpit as I stared out at these dear friends I had visited in hospitals and whose loved ones I had buried. They wept with me, but they also graciously encouraged me to move on to "bigger and better things" since they were just "a washed-up bunch of old folks."

Why would they feel like washed-up old folks? Maybe because churches full of young people put ads on billboards like "Not Your Aunt Gertrude's Church."

I left for something "bigger," I suppose, but "bigger" has nothing to do with "better."

Disappointment in the cultural irrelevance of the church is justifiable. But much of the disappointment may stem as much from a culturally conditioned arrogance as from a sincere commitment to missional, crosscultural living. When we younger adults rail against the Christian subculture of primarily older generations for their narrow-minded cultural illiteracy, we often fail to notice that we are ourselves part of a subculture with its own narrowness and cultural ignorance. We seem to suppose that anyone who can't quote lines from *The Office* or lyrics from Wilco is out of touch.

But maybe Aunt Gertrude is not so out of touch. To be out of touch with that particular slice of society to whom Michael Scott's awkward antics on *The Office* have such appeal is not to be out of touch with *everyone*. There are other slices of American culture made up of folks who have never heard Arcade Fire playing on a coffee bar's satellite radio station while sipping a latte.

Since I have spent time in pastoral ministry among both twenty-somethings and eighty-somethings, and since my readers will generally fall within the former category than the latter, I want to take extra space in this chapter to critique the cynicism of young people toward the church's cultural irrelevance. If you want to read more about the church's cultural irrelevance, you can check Amazon or scan the shelves of the local bookshop—they are now "legion."

It is important for those of us in the younger generations to step far enough back from our own cultural milieu to observe that the marketing power directed our way is staggering and quite disproportionate to the size of our subculture. (Corporate execs know we are less careful with our money.) Is it possible that all this attention from Hollywood, Apple, the music industry and online networking companies has spoiled us to the point that we have now become rather high maintenance, demanding lavish catering from the wider church? (If I can download multiple apps to my smartphone, then why can't the local church give me what I want?)

Christians must become more adept at reaching the younger generations, but are those of us in those younger generations willing and able to reciprocate and bridge the cultural lines of our elders? Are we striving to understand the struggles of those in their mid-forties rearing teenagers? Are we making strides to relate to the loneliness of empty-nest divorcées? Are we able to express genuine interest in the news programs and game shows that feature in the living rooms of our grandparents? Are we willing to venture out into the cultural realm of retirees or learn from that diminishing number of WWII veterans?

Are we too hip to worship with Aunt Gertrude?

It is noted at times that younger Christians are more in tune with culture and more familiar with society's technological innovations. But maybe culture-savvy twenty-seven-year-olds are really only savvy about their own particular subsection of society. Or maybe they are only so culture-savvy because they have more time to watch TV and surf the Internet than a forty-seven-year-old with teenagers and aging parents.

I think older Christians, specifically older ministers, have so much to learn from the younger leaders of the church. (Earl Crepps has written a book called *Reverse Mentoring* that can serve as a guide in the process.)[5] Personally, I have learned so much from listening to my younger brothers and sisters in the faith. The Bible even promotes a certain degree of this didactic reversal. The impressively trained Pharisees should have listened more carefully to those little kids praising Jesus in the temple ("out of the mouth of infants and nursing babies / you have prepared praise" [Matthew 21:16; cf. Psalm 8:2]), and there is certainly a pattern of the older serving the younger in the Genesis patriarchal narratives. But the biblical tradition of young men and women respecting their elders is also a persistent theme. After all, "honor your father and your mother" made it into the Ten Commandments (Exodus 20:12; Deuteronomy 5:16) and much of the material in Proverbs is presented as parental instruction to the young. The reason God's people existed as a divided kingdom (Israel in the north and Judah in the south) was because Solomon's rash young son Rehoboam refused to heed the wisdom of his elders: "He abandoned the counsel that the old men gave him and took counsel with the young men who had grown up with him and stood before him" (1 Kings 12:8). He listened to the arrogant advice of his peers and saw the kingdom ripped apart before his youthful eyes—an ancient case, perhaps, of cultural arrogance.

THE CYNICAL RESPONSE OF CULTURAL ASSIMILATION

I have a great deal of respect for Cameron Strang and Relevant Media Group. The success of *Relevant* magazine evidences the widespread hunger among twenty- and thirty-somethings for an intelligent Christian forum that understands and appreciates their subculture. When I was on *Relevant*'s website (www.relevantmagazine.com) recently, I noticed that one of the words used by an outside publishing company to market a book to *Relevant*'s young readership was *irreverent.* Publishers know that the more snarky, edgy and cynical a product is, the more likely young Christians will whip out their credit cards and make the purchase.

In a cynical market, irreverence sells.

The danger of cultural relevance is always cultural assimilation. This is when we become *like* the world in order to *win* the world. Christianity must engage society, but history has shown us that our faith loses its vivacity and integrity once it becomes infiltrated with the outside culture. In *unChristian*, Kinnaman and Lyons point out that "young people are significantly less likely than older adults to limit their media content out of a discomfort with the values or perspectives represented."[7] If we are going to insist that the church cater more to our cultural preferences as young people, then we need to be carefully examining whether or not those cultural preferences are actually biblical. To what extent are we unhealthily influenced by the dangerous elements of our media-saturated subculture? When Christian publishers start posting words like *irreverent* on Christian websites to advertise Christian books, then something is amiss. Do we really want the church to become relevant to those aspects of our youthful subculture we may have embraced carelessly and uncritically?

We don't need to exchange irrelevance for irreverence.

John's Gospel is particularly concerned that we understand Jesus' teaching that Christians are newly sourced in a realm markedly dissimilar from this world. In John 17 Jesus prayed,

> I have given them your word, and the world has hated them because they are not of the world, just as I am not of the world. I do not ask that you take them out of the world, but that you keep them from the evil one. They are not of the world, just as I am not of the world. (John 17:14-16)

The phrase "in but not of the world" seems to come from passages like this. The point is that followers of Christ are born "from above" (John 3:3, 7) and thus definitively dissociated from the realm of the "world" (a term appearing almost eighty times in John).[8] Yet we are to remain "witnesses" (another favorite Johannine word) to Jesus as we remain *in* the world (seeking cultural relevance) while not being *of* the world (resisting cultural assimilation).

Though Jesus and Paul stand as New Testament witnesses to the need for cultural relevance, they also demonstrate the need for being *countercultural*. The mission of God's kingdom requires that we insightfully *engage* culture while presenting a message that will inevitably *challenge* culture. The escapism of cultural irrelevance is not to be replaced with the conformism of cultural assimilation:

> We have no liberty to preserve our holiness by escaping from the world, or to sacrifice our holiness by conforming to the world. Escapism and conformism are both forbidden to us.[9]

Those of us committed to communicating the gospel to younger, more cynical generations must heed the wisdom of Henri Nouwen, who wrote that one of the greatest temptations Christian leaders will face is the temptation to be *relevant*.[10] Being culturally relevant to a fallen culture is not exactly the goal, is it? Nouwen writes, "I am convinced that the Christian leader of the future is called to be completely irrelevant and to stand in this world with nothing to offer but his or her own vulnerable self."[11]

I don't think Nouwen would tell us to rig locking mechanisms onto the church basketball hoops or to put down our copies of *Relevant* magazine. But Nouwen was keenly sensitive to the pressure to accommodate to our culture in a way that compromises authentic Christianity. We must offer that which transcends all cultural preferences: genuine human relationships that reflect the gospel and the love of Christ. Is this something jaded young cynics can offer?

CROWD, CLIQUE OR COMMUNITY?

Crowds are large groups of people with a shared external focus but little internal coherence. Cliques are small groups of people with a strong internal coherence but virtually no external focus. Churches should be neither. Crowds are drawn to the culturally relevant, so crowd ministries are susceptible to cultural assimilation. Cliques, on the other hand, have no outward orientation and thus become bastions of irrelevant churchianity.

When Jesus began his ministry in Galilee, great crowds followed. There were no blog posts or tweets, but word has always seemed to travel fast when it comes to the spectacular—the rumors were spreading that a messiah figure with the power to heal illnesses was on the march. Though he eyed those multitudes with the compassion of a loving shepherd, when it came to the attention they gave him, Jesus was ambivalent, sometimes even evasive. Wherever large crowds appeared, Jesus seemed to eventually disappear. He did not come to reshape the people of God into a faceless crowd fascinated with the latest religious fads or with the shock and awe of the miraculous.

Too many of our churches seem to be mere crowds. Every Sunday nameless masses gather together with the external foci of a dynamic speaker and an impressive worship band that attempt to offer church-flavored yet culturally relevant experiences. But then the masses trickle out of the multiple parking lots and fade into the suburban landscape with little sense of internal connectivity to one another as constituent parts of a family.

When that internal connectivity is strong, however, it is easy for churches to become cliques. In this case, inward interaction is often exciting and comfortable, regardless of who is preaching or how tight the choir or the worship band sounds. But Jesus did not come to form cliques. Sure, he selectively handpicked a crew of disciples to become his intimate understudies, but this was a very temporary arrangement, and he was known to send them out on special assignments that surely kept their vision from becoming too provincially limited to an inner circle.

The disciples were most clique-ish immediately following the resurrection and ascension. In both cases they were found nestled together as a "holy huddle" in that upper room. Until, that is, Jesus' Spirit took up residence in their midst and flung open the doors. The holy huddle spilled out into the Jerusalem streets on Pentecost. They were boisterous and noisy with the praises of God in the public square. The church became the church when it stopped being a clique.

Crowds are so externally focused on someone or some impressive phenomenon that they fail to grow relationally with one another. Sustaining a crowd usually requires some degree of catering to cultural interests. Cliques are externally blind yet so inwardly directed that they can become stagnant. Sustaining a clique demands social strictures to be kept so airtight that potential participants are kept on the outside. A *biblical community*, however, maintains an inward health along with outward vision. What we find in the early pages of the book of Acts is a church that promotes not only a profound sense of cohesion with powerful inner dynamics but also a vigorous outreach to their surrounding environs. When the internal and external em-

phases become imbalanced, we then find churchianity (like the Thessalonians) or cultural assimilation (like the Corinthians).

The church's struggle between cultural irrelevance and cultural assimilation goes back to its inception, forming much of the basis for the
Epistles that were eventually canonized as Scripture. Today, our
megachurches must work to provide environments that develop internal relationships. Smaller churches that enjoy loving fellowship with
one another must vigilantly resist the tendency to neglect the neighbors living in anonymity just around the corner. We do not need any
more culturally assimilated crowds or culturally irrelevant cliques.
We need biblical communities.

LEARNING FROM MOUNT HERMON BAPTIST CHURCH

Serving folks who were mostly in their sixties to eighties, with some
in their nineties, and between six years of working with eighteen- to
twenty-two-year-olds has afforded an interesting vantage point for
learning lessons from both young and old. There is a great deal that
Mount Hermon Baptist Church and the Aunt Gertrudes of the world
can learn from the college students I have been working with. However, because I anticipate a younger readership, I thought it would be
helpful to close this chapter by listing a few areas where we could
learn a great deal from our elders!

1. Loyalty and devotion. With the divorce rate so high, leading a
young couple in their marriage vows comes with a degree of trepidation.
I had no such trepidation, however, with Buddy and Jo, because when I
officiated their wedding, it was on their sixtieth anniversary—they
wanted to celebrate six decades of devotion to one another by renewing
those holy vows. With all the breakups and relationship drama among
young people in our society, it would probably do us a lot of good to
forgo the *Friends* reruns and spend some time with a man and a woman
who have persevered in an imperfect yet decades-long marriage.

Along with marital devotion, our elders are usually much more
devoted to consistent church involvement. There were two men at
Mount Hermon who literally risked life and limb to show up for

worship. One of them had to pace himself to keep from losing his breath as he traversed the long, painful thirty yards from the parking lot to the sanctuary. Another gentleman had to begin getting into his suit two hours before the service to make sure he had enough time to regain his energy for the two-mile drive to the church. I think of these two men when college students sleep in on Sunday mornings or decide not to attend a Bible study because of a TV show.

Loyalty and devotion to the church was so strong that a handful of Mount Hermon's parishioners loyally came to church even when they got nothing out of the music or the messages. One fellow would sometimes take my hand, look at me as best he could through his cataracts, and say, "Well young man, I couldn't hear a word of that sermon, but I could sure tell you meant it." I think of this dear soul when younger folks unknowingly approach church with the consumer mentality that asks, What can I get out of this service?

2. Community. I talk a great deal about community, but I really don't want you to inconvenience me with a poorly timed phone call or, heaven forbid, a drop-in visit.

As much buzz as there is among younger generations on building genuine community, we actually have a rather low tolerance for the awkward, slow work required for building true intimacy. Many of our elders may be much better at this type of work than we are. They are certainly more prepared for the length of time required for building community, and they may also have better instincts for which environments work best for deepening relationships. When the folks at Mount Hermon called on the phone, they took their time in conversation. And since phone conversations are inferior to face-to-face encounters, they would get into their cars and drive to someone's house to sit around a well-used living room. In contrast, there have been a number of times when a distraught college student would be in my office describing painful misunderstandings with a friend before I eventually discovered that their most recent conversations were conducted via the computer or by text messaging.

I remember moving to a small town and having to get used to visitors dropping in and messing up my plans for watching the news or having a quiet supper with my wife. In recent reflection on those interruptions, I have been reminded of how my grandparents hosted drop-in guests. My grandfather always had an infinite amount of farm work awaiting him, but those guests never departed without hearing him say, "Now, don't hurry." Restaurants and coffee shops are great places to meet friends and hang out, but there is nothing like a warm slice of homemade pound cake with a glass of milk at someone's kitchen table.

3. A sense of mortality. Something else I learned from the folks at Mount Hermon is that nothing builds community like the pain of sickness and death. Relationships reach new depths of intimacy when we visit someone confined to a hospital bed. On countless occasions I took the elevators at Durham Regional, Chapel Hill and Duke University Hospitals to visit and pray for church members who had fallen ill. When a twenty-three-year-old nurse has to bring your dinner with a straw, it serves as a convincing reminder that we are no more than "a mist that appears for a little time and then vanishes" (James 4:14). Many young people, however, maintain a sense of invincibility, which obscures the reality that our every breath hangs on the sovereign power of God.

Older Christians have much to learn from their younger brothers and sisters in the faith, as well as the other way around. We are not going to learn very much from each other, however, if we never spend time together, and I know of no context other than Sunday mornings in church sanctuaries where young and old are extended the opportunity to be together in the same time and same place. Maybe cultural irrelevance will gradually fade away if the culture-savvy youngsters would become more actively involved in the messy and inconvenient subculture of church life.

DISCUSSION QUESTIONS

1. Name some ways that you think churches are out of touch with the culture around them.

2. Who do you believe has more to learn from the other: the younger or older generations? Explain.

3. What are some ways that the older and younger generations can begin to merge in their journeys toward Christ? Give specific examples.

4. Can you identify times when you have been sheltered from the culture around you by a bubble of churchianity?

5. Name your three closest friends who are not Christians. (If you can't easily do this, then perhaps you are in more of a Christian bubble than you realize.)

6. Identify some ways you have become unbiblically *too* much like the culture around you.

part two

BIBLICAL ALTERNATIVES TO CYNICISM

Are there responses to pop Christianity besides cynicism that can promote healing in the church? Can we be discerning Christians without becoming full-blown cynics? Is there a way to critique and challenge the church more out of love than out of disgust?

These questions appeared in the introduction, and I answered with "yes."

A more complicated question also appeared in the introduction: Could there be a form of cynicism that is beneficial and perhaps even *biblical?*

For so many serious questions the lines are quite fine and the slopes are so slippery that it is difficult to make clear-cut affirmations. In the biblical passages that feature throughout this next major section of the book we will find sharp disillusionment, bitter anger and intense frustration. There will be wry satire and despairing cries. We are about to discover that many of the biblical figures that challenged God's people (and sometimes God himself) have much in common with contemporary cynics.

So, can cynicism be biblical? In spite of the fine lines and the slippery slopes, I venture to answer no. Though the prophets, sages and poets of Israel exhibit much in common with the cynicism we see directed toward God and the church today, their indignation and misery were ultimately more *con*structive than *de*structive. The despair and fury are not to be blunted or dismissed, but it must be acknowledged that their ministries were ultimately grounded in the unfolding drama of God's redemption and restoration of all things. The ranting and raving of either Job or Jeremiah could give our fiercest contemporary cynics a run for their money. But the canonical witness of their stories within the wider story of the Bible nudges us toward a hopefulness premised on the belief, however faint it may be in dark times, that there is a righteous Lord who will make all things right—one day.

Hopeful realism is the phrase I am using to distinguish the biblical examples of Israel's prophets, sages and poets, along with Jesus and the apostle Paul, from what we recognize as cynicism in the church today. The line between cynicism and hopeful realism will appear blurred at times. Distinguishing features include the *direction* and the *source* of the indignation and disappointment. When the disillusionment is expressed in the direction of praise and eschatological hopefulness, and when the dismay is sourced in love for God and for his people, then we can begin to sketch out a demarcation line between a cynic and a hopeful realist.

Along with the questions that first appeared in the introduction, I also affirmed there that redeemed cynics have much to offer the church. Since disillusionment is illumination—the (often painful) dispersal of illusion—cynics have much to offer the church if they can do so in love and in the direction of hope and praise. By pointing out the inappropriate responses of cynics in the previous chapters on pop Christianity, I am not suggesting that we just grit our teeth and ignore the church's misconceptions. The hopeful realists in this section of the book will provide a number of scriptural ways to address false notions and faulty practices.

We will begin with the biblical prophets who were anti-institutional and profoundly opposed to the religiosity of their day. The biblical sages come next. They provided their ancient society with not only wisdom but also with corrective critiques of the oversimplification and misuse of wisdom. Next, we will take a look at Israel's mournful poets. Prophets and sages certainly produced poetry. But of special importance for this section of the book are those poets who were courageous enough to produce the raw, angst-riddled songs of lament. We are in search of biblical models not only for disabusing the people of God of their dangerous delusions, but also for biblical means by which we can, like those tragic poets, address God himself when *he* is behind the reasons for our disillusionment. The agonizing laments of the psalmists and the critiques provided by the sages and prophets provide us with instructive patterns and modes for engaging both God and the church in our frustrations.

Yet these prophets, sages and poets are not to be esteemed as perfect models. Once someone is presented in Scripture as remarkably heroic, we suddenly find them eyeing Bathsheba from a rooftop, or deflated and forlorn beneath a broom tree, or absconding from the Gentile section of the dinner table in Antioch. We can, however, read the vocational patterns set forward in the prophetic, wisdom and lament literature and find much to emulate. For an unflawed role model for addressing God and his people in disappointment and dismay, we have only one we can turn to. So following the chapters on the prophets, sages and tragic poets, we will consider the ministry of Jesus, who came to suffer divine abandonment on behalf of a wayward people misguided and deluded by all sorts of pop religious ideas. Of all the leaders of both Israel and the church, no one has had more reason to cynically give up on the people of God than the Messiah, and yet no one gave so much. Of all the leaders who found themselves seemingly rejected by God after embracing a divine summons to service, no one had more reason to shake a cynical fist heavenward, yet no one obeyed so fully.

8

the way of
the prophet

Prophetic Anguish Instead of Cynical Anger

*If we are to understand prophetic criticism,
we must see that its characteristic
idiom is anguish, not anger.*

—Walter Brueggemann, *The Prophetic Imagination*

*This is the burden of a prophet: compassion for man
and sympathy for God.*

—Abraham Heschel, *The Prophets*

*As an example of suffering and patience, brothers,
take the prophets who spoke in the name of the Lord.*

James 5:10

The biblical prophets made fierce, abrasive protests against injustice and religiosity, with the spiritual and political leaders of God's people receiving the brunt of the blasts. Such corrective voices are urgently needed among God's people today. Our churches are beset with moral failures, internal rivalries and with theological distortions of the sort described in the first half of this book. Irresponsibility and neglect must be confronted. Audacious delusions about faith must be exposed. Dissenting voices are needed to cry out against the corruption, to censure the vain pursuits, to defy the deplorable status quo. Start shouting, please . . . someone.

But not just anyone.

The shrill voice of the prophet is easily confused with the shrill voice of the cynic. Both can be abrasive. Both can be accurate in their accusations. The fine line between the two can be discerned when we realize that God intends to vocalize his admonishing words through those who share not only in his *disgust* but also in his *love*. The abrasive voice that decries the error of God's people without God's heart for his people, and without a hopefulness that God will somehow reorder all things, is not the voice of a *prophet* but the voice of a *cynic*.

PROPHET OR CYNIC?

"You need to do something about this. What has happened is wrong and you know it, so get out there on that campus and tell the world. You need to demand the president's resignation."

This is a brief excerpt from the first of many impassioned exhortations I have received from students while working in campus ministry. Gary was furiously annoyed over the scandalous news flash that the president of our Christian university had purportedly altered a star athlete's grade to satisfy NCAA academic eligibility requirements. Within weeks of entering my first full-time ministry post since seminary I found myself in the midst of a brouhaha that proved newsworthy enough to draw reporters from the *New York Times*.

"You are one of the spiritual leaders of this campus, and you need to make a stand." Gary was giving me a chance to demonstrate that I had a backbone.

The university was harshly divided. Certain departments were rising to the president's defense while others were angrily demanding his dismissal. My supervisor was the minister to the university, and we had agreed to maintain a neutral stance. The initial details were incomplete and inconsistent—we did not want to take sides prematurely. (We also respected the authority of the presidential office and did not view lightly the path of professional mutiny!)

"It does not matter if he signs your paychecks. What's wrong is wrong."

The more I listened to this young man's tirade against injustice and the abuse of power behind closed presidential doors, the more I became convinced that Gary might be right. He wanted me to leave the safety of my office and join him and the other students who were protesting out on the street corner. Shouldn't he expect that I would cry out with an abrasive voice in righteous dismay against apparent injustice?

Yes—and no.

There was another reason why I had agreed with my supervisor to delay in taking a side. He had wisely perceived that prematurely standing in opposition to or in support of the president would compromise our ability to minister to those in the other camp. I explained this ministerial concern to Gary, but what he wanted from us was not a pastoral strategy. He wanted a prophetic protest.

This raised a red flag for me. I admired his passion and fortitude that morning in my office, but I had to wonder if he was more motivated by a disgust with the institution than by a love for the community. He wanted "The Man" pinned to the wall, come what may to the divided, disillusioned masses for whom my supervisor and I had some degree of pastoral responsibility. God can be rough around the edges, especially when justice is at stake, but was the abrasiveness in Gary's voice sourced in divine indignation or in his personal distrust of the system?

Another red flag was raised with my realization that this was the first time I had ever met Gary, even though campus ministry events had been well underway. I eventually learned that he was a cynical, anti-institutional religious studies major who had distanced himself from the student ministry community on campus. He had some really strong points during our discussion that day, but I had to struggle to discern if I was listening to the harsh voice of a *prophet* or of a *cynic*. Making such distinctions is no easy task.

Gary left my office disappointed with me—I made the decision to maintain the neutral stance until more information was provided. The angry cynicism I detected made me hesitant to accept his advice to join in the grass-roots protest movement. But I also detected the burdensome anguish of a prophet in Gary. A few days later, when I was asked to stand at the president's side as he sought to clear his name before student forums, I refused. Gary had inspired me.

The purpose of this chapter is to delineate the differences between "the way of the prophet" and "the way of the cynic," commending the former as an appropriate and biblical means of addressing ethical wrongs and theological delusions within the church. Before studying the contrasts between the two, it will be helpful to review the nature of prophetic ministry found in the pages of the Old Testament.

THE OLD TESTAMENT PROPHETIC TRADITION

"Samuel, we want a king. All the other nations have a king. We want one, too" (see 1 Samuel 8:5). This demand made by Israel's elders was not received well by the old prophet. Why? Because they already had a King. Since the exodus, Israel had existed as a loose confederation of tribal groups under the royal headship of God himself. They now wanted to exchange a *theocracy* for a *monarchy*: "And the LORD said to Samuel, 'Obey the voice of the people in all that they say to you, for they have not rejected you, but they have rejected me from being king over them'" (1 Samuel 8:7).

And so began a multicentury epoch that can be viewed as one of the darkest hours in biblical history.

The Hebrew monarchy began with Saul. He turned out to be a disappointment rather early in his career, so God eventually had him replaced with a young shepherd-warrior who hailed from the little town of Bethlehem. In spite of the initial bad start, the monarchy idea gained some validity as David demonstrated loyalty to God and established Israel as a local superpower. His military victories cleared the way for the economic and political stability that permitted the architectural and cultural renaissance led by his son Solomon. Though endowed with matchless wisdom, it did not take long for Solomon to destabilize the nation and consign it to a downward trajectory.

The kingdom was split into two realms—Israel in the north and the smaller Judah in the south. After two centuries of rather pathetic monarchs, the Northern Kingdom plummeted deeper and deeper into spiritual rot. They neglected the ideals of societal justice prescribed in the law and embraced idolatrous religious practices, including cult prostitution and even child sacrifice. This madness came to an abrupt end when the pagan Assyrians destroyed Israel's capital city of Samaria in 722 B.C. and brutally drove the citizens into the shame and disorientation of exile.

Judah fared more nobly under the leadership of David's dynasty until Israel's vile practices began to spread southward like a spiritual contagion. In spite of the commendable leadership of later kings like Hezekiah and Josiah, the Southern Kingdom began speeding with locomotive force into its own disastrous demise. Painfully etched into Jewish memory is the date 586 B.C., when the Babylonian king Nebuchadnezzar smashed through Jerusalem's walls, ripped down Solomon's temple, and deported more of God's people into exile.

Throughout this tragic saga, God's arms were opened wide to his people, urging their return at the behest of the prophets:

> Yet the LORD warned Israel and Judah by every prophet and every seer, saying, "Turn from your evil ways and keep my commandments and my statutes, in accordance with all the Law that I commanded your fathers, and that I sent to you by my servants the prophets." But they would not listen. (2 Kings 17:13-14)

The writings of the biblical prophets open a vista not only on a dark epoch of Israel's past but also reveal a side of God that many of us would prefer to never see. In their written oracles we encounter a God who "roars" (Amos 1:2), a God whose "way is in whirlwind and storm" (Nahum 1:3). He is not only tempestuously enraged but also crushed and grieved, suffering the pangs of heartache while nevertheless longing to extend mercy: "My heart recoils within me; / my compassion grows warm and tender" (Hosea 11:8). The prophetic literature affords us a glimpse of God as both irate and heart-stricken.

The tension of these divine emotions was expressed to Israel and Judah through these prophets. They shouted, their castigating voices demanding repentance and reform among a people plagued with deaf ears. There were certainly predictive elements in their messages, but contrary to popular understandings of the biblical prophets, they did not function merely as ancient fortunetellers. For the most part the Old Testament prophet addressed immediate situations for which God had a defining word. Prophetic ministry is the outcry of God through his servants in specific situations of life.

When Amos writes that God "does nothing / without revealing his secret / to his servants the prophets" (Amos 3:7), he is affirming that our God is a God of means. God conducts much of his work in this world via human agency, vocalizing his protest against injustice and error through faithful servants. Though there is no formally designated leadership office of "prophet" in contemporary Christianity, the church's need for prophetic ministry is just as dire today as it was during the days of Isaiah or Zephaniah.

The problem we have been wrestling with is that the prophetic voice sounds so similar to the cynical voice. Both can be shrill. Both utilize satire and offer incisive critiques. Both are sounded from the periphery of church life. We will consider this shared post out on the periphery and then strive to understand the differences between the prophet and the cynic by studying a few distinguishing contrasts: engagement versus disengagement, sympathy versus apathy, and anguish versus anger.

ON THE FRINGES: THE PROPHETIC SCHOOL
AND THE CYNICAL ANTICOMMUNITY

Nineveh? Jonah was annoyed. *Of all the cities in the world, God wants me to go to Nineveh?* This was the capital city of Assyria, one of the most ruthless, barbaric empires of the ancient world. They had been harassing God's people for decades. Jonah was no fool—he knew what this "gracious" and "merciful" God had up his sleeve (Jonah 4:2). If the Ninevites received his preaching, they would be forgiven. Jonah wanted no part in a peace mission to an oppressing nation.

So off to the far-flung fringes of the ancient world: "Yes, captain, I would like a one-way ticket for Tarshish—keep the shekels."

That plan did not work out so well. By way of a circuitous and perilous route, Jonah ended up on Assyrian shores covered in whale digestive funk. Reluctantly, he preached up and down those pagan streets, and to his displeasure the Ninevites repented. Jonah smugly retreated to the fringes once more—the outskirts of the great city—though he remained within range to observe what God would do, hoping for fire and brimstone in spite of the positive reception of his message.

Among the biblical prophets Jonah is the one most certainly *not* presented as a role model. He is portrayed as "an anti-hero, at cross purposes with Yahweh who sent him" and as one whose name is associated with "the expansion for the realm of the wicked reign of Jeroboam II" (see 2 Kings 14:24-25).[1] Throughout this short story we find Jonah continually creating distance not only between himself and God but also between himself and those God sent him to.

This is not the way of the prophet. This is the way of the cynic.

Prophets and cynics do, however, share this similar space along the outskirts. Due to their abrasive messages, they both end up marginalized. How they get to the periphery differs—prophets are usually shoved there by others, and cynics, like Jonah, usually rush to the fringes on their own accord.

During the days of Elijah and Elisha there was a school of prophets dwelling in remote areas due to political persecution. Certain groups of false prophets happily delivered oracles that tickled the royal ear of the king, but those whose voices were faithfully fractious were unwelcome in the public square and relegated to the fringes. Elijah's vocational hazards repeatedly compelled him to seek refuge in wilderness regions or in Gentile territory. When Jezebel began programmatically destroying Yahweh worship, prophets became an endangered species. A fellow named Obadiah found one hundred of them for whom he provided the safe haven of a cave. Years later the priest at Bethel during the reign of King Jeroboam II (with whom Jonah may be associated, at least in a literary sense if not in a historical sense) told Amos to leave town and take his inconvenient oracles elsewhere. A century later we encounter Jeremiah, perhaps the most unwanted prophet to walk the streets of Jerusalem (until Jesus, at least). The false prophets who happily declared "peace, peace" (Jeremiah 6:14; 8:11; cf. Ezekiel 13:10, 16) when there was no peace were heartily received in the royal court and on the temple steps. The prophets true to God were such nuisances that they were tossed to the fringes.

The fringe existence of cynics, however, is often self-appointed. Today's disgruntled believers who are trying to find somewhere to nurse (or flaunt) their disillusionment will likely find themselves uncomfortable among the sunny faces of Sunday morning worship services. Religiously disenchanted yet spiritually inclined, they reposition themselves on the outer rim of institutional Christianity, where they can breathe a bit more freely and enjoy controversial conversation without reprisal. From this safe distance, Christian cynics enjoy raising religious eyebrows. Fringe life provides enough proximity for observing ridiculous behavior in the church and enough distance for criticizing such behavior safely. Jonah's perch beyond Nineveh's walls provided him a convenient location as a spectator of Nineveh's (hopefully dreadful) fate.

Christian cynics can be loners, but for the most part they tend to congregate together. More attractive than the fellowship offered by the institutional church are social networks of other believers who share religious disenchantment as a common bond. When these com-

anti something

munities become launching pads for attack rather than sanctuaries for healing from the pains of disillusionment, they may be described as "anticommunities." Like any community, the cynical anticommunity provides relationships and a place of belonging to its members, but it is a community defined not so much by what it is *for* but by what it is *against*. The anticommunity may be the kids who sit in the back of the room during youth group and make fun of the activities or Bible studies. It may be the group of Christian college students who take collective pride in using profanity and blaring secular music. It could be the group of retirees who prefer to meet not at the local church on Sundays but at the local coffee shop or bar to discuss the latest outlandish comments made by religious, right-wing political candidates. These informal social networks of cynical believers are never far removed from the established faith community—their professed allegiance to Christ keeps them within arm's length of the church, while their cynicism keeps them distant enough to lob critiques from afar.

ARMS CROSSED OR OUTSTRETCHED?
PROPHETIC ENGAGEMENT VERSUS CYNICAL DISTANCE

Those of us who find ourselves out on the fringes of faith communities must make a choice concerning our *posture* on the fringes. The choice of cynics is to turn their backs to the church in disgust. Prophets are called to stretch out their arms in love.

We have seen that although Jonah's plans to escape to the fringes of the known world were aborted (he never made it to Tarshish), he still managed to resort to fringe life just east of Nineveh, even after the mass revival that resulted from his preaching. From that distance he sulked and complained, angry that God had shown mercy. This seems parallel to the way of the Christian cynic, who often derides the church at a volitional distance with arms crossed. Alternatively, the way of the faithful prophet is to make protest at an enforced distance with arms outstretched.

The biblical prophets were terribly disgusted with human failure, and they had to personally wrestle with theological truths that rattled and disturbed them. Even so, the disgust and frustration were not accepted as excuses for disengaging themselves from God or his people. It was certainly a temptation. Elijah seemed ready to turn in his prophetic mantle and die under that broom tree (1 Kings 19). Isaiah was instructed to proclaim truth to those who would never embrace his message (Isaiah 6). Jeremiah may have wanted to run, but he found himself unable to abandon his sorrowful mission of preaching God's word—"I am weary with holding it in, / and I cannot" (Jeremiah 20:9). They did not take jibes and critical shots at Judah or Israel while seated comfortably on the fringes with their prophet cronies. Instead, they were nudged by God to keep plodding from the fringes to engage those to whom they were sent.

WEEPING OR SNEERING? PROPHETIC SYMPATHY
VERSUS CYNICAL APATHY
Confrontation is a part of Christian ministry. It is most fruitfully received when it comes from someone who loves us and who is emotionally invested in our welfare. Wouldn't we prefer to be confronted by someone for whom the task is unpleasant and difficult? How annoying it is to be confronted by someone who actually delights in correcting us!

It does not appear as though the prophets cracked derisive smiles when they vocalized God's disappointment. They often exhibited sympathy and were at times personally grieved over the pain and turmoil of their tough messages. Though shoved to the fringes, they were called to embrace and even embody the plights of the people they served, occasionally identifying with forthcoming national sufferings by way of symbolic actions: Jeremiah strapped a yoke to his back to symbolize the coming lordship of the Babylonian king Nebuchadnezzar (Jeremiah 27); Ezekiel laid on his side eating food baked over dung to personally represent the siege of Jerusalem (Ezekiel 4); the New Testament prophet Agabus bound his hands and feet with a belt to show Paul the fate awaiting him (Acts 21). These dramatic actions served as visible means of instruction and required the prophet to physically identify with the impending misery of God's people.

Even when the prophets did not overtly sympathize with the misery of their hearers (Jeremiah was told at certain moments not even to intercede for them! [Jeremiah 7:16; 11:14; 14:11-12]), they were nonetheless called to sympathize with the misery of God himself. The call to prophetic service was an invitation into the violent rage and the crushing grief of the heart of God. Hosea's marriage to a prostitute was a participation in the heartache God experienced in his betrothal to Israel, who had become as an adulterous bride. Beckoned into this "divine pathos,"[2] the prophets squirmed, wept and howled in both the grief and the wrath of God:

> I will lament and wail;
>   I will go stripped and naked;
> I will make lamentation like the jackals,
>   and mourning like the ostriches. (Micah 1:8)

The story of Jonah opens with his decision to flee "from the presence of the LORD" (Jonah 1:3). The story closes with God asking him the pointed question: "should I not pity Nineveh?" (Jonah 4:11). This "prophet" disengaged himself by fleeing from God and then refused to demonstrate compassion for those he was sent to. There is no sympathy for either God or the Ninevites, only an apathy that soon intensified to become downright antipathy. Jonah would have been quite pleased to be in Tarshish, "away" from God, thank you very much, and he would have enjoyed the spectacle of heaven spitting fire on Nineveh.

Among the spiritually cynical, it is in vogue to not care, to be disaffected and disinterested, to laugh at the church rather than to weep for the church. Disillusionment often results in disengagement, and to be disengaged is to be apathetic—we tend to lack concern and compassion when we are hurt and annoyed. It is difficult to care for those who frustrate us. It is difficult to care about a belief system that seems to have left us empty. Without a vested interest in the health of the church, cynics sneer at the shortcomings and tragedies in organized

Christianity rather than plodding from the fringes into the fray to somehow bring salutary correction. There is an absence of pathos (apathy) rather than a participation in the pathos (sympathy). And sometimes apathy is simply the prelude to a cruel antipathy that delights in seeing the bubbles burst (or the city consumed with fire from the sky).

TORTURED OR TORTURING? PROPHETIC ANGUISH VERSUS CYNICAL ANGER

It is not that cynics lack any feelings whatsoever, but whereas prophets must be gripped by the pathos of the One who has called them, cynics can become obsessed with their own personal pathos. What some cynics may play off as sophisticated inward turmoil may be no more than begrudging self-pity. Remember, cynicism is like a sickness resulting from spiritual wounds becoming infected, from brokenness souring into bitterness. It also results in *anguish* turning into *anger*.

Is anger ever justified? Or as God phrased the question to Jonah, "Do you do well to be angry?" (Jonah 4:4). God is certainly presented as angry in the prophetic writings, but this is not a temperament he adopts eagerly or impulsively—in contrast to his own heated ire, Jonah had just proclaimed that God is actually "slow to anger" (Jonah 4:2), a common description of God throughout the Old Testament (see also James 1:19). When God is angry with his children, it is not divorced from compassionate grief. Reading Hosea is a bumpy journey through the conflicting emotions of One who is not only full of wrath but also full of longing for his wayward people. So, do we do well to be angry? Jonah was mad because God had permitted the repentance of the Ninevites and because he had lost that fine shade tree God had given him. This is an example of what James calls "the anger of man," which "does not produce the righteousness that God requires" (James 1:20). Only if our anger is sourced in the slow and conflicted anger of God is it justified (see chap. 9).

The tension between love and wrath, compassion and anger, is expressed in the term used by Old Testament scholar Walter Bruegge-

mann to describe the characteristic emotion of the prophet: *anguish*.[3]
The prophets seem to have been tortured souls who were ever striving
to resist bitterness without denying the pain of brokenness. This
struggle is portrayed poignantly in Jeremiah, whose personal frustration and misery were so acute that he lamented his own birth (Jeremiah 15:10; 20:14-18), prayed that God would exact vengeance on his
enemies (Jeremiah 15:15), and accused God of deceiving him (Jeremiah 20:7).[4] Even so, he was also wracked with tremendous concern
for his people, suffering violently on their behalf:

> My joy is gone; grief is upon me;
> > my heart is sick within me. . . .
> For the wound of the daughter of my people is my heart
> > wounded. (Jeremiah 8:18, 21)

When reading Jeremiah, I find it hard to distinguish between his
voice and God's in some of his oracles. This may be because he was so
intimately participating in the divine pathos that their voices became
synonymous:

> My anguish, my anguish! I writhe in pain!
> > Oh the walls of my heart!
> My heart is beating wildly;
> > I cannot keep silent,
> for I hear the sound of the trumpet,
> > the alarm of war.
> Crash follows hard on crash;
> > the whole land is laid waste.
> Suddenly my tents are laid waste,
> > my curtains in a moment. (Jeremiah 4:19-20)

Are cynics so united with the grief of God's own heart that their
voices blend with his? Such a mysterious confluence of both divine
and prophetic anguish comes to its fullest expression on the cross,
where God's love and wrath collide in the paradigmatic prophetic
ministry of Jesus. "The cross is the assurance that effective prophetic

criticism is done not by an outsider but always by one who must embrace the grief, enter into the death, and know the pain of the criticized one."[5] With these words Brueggemann is exhorting all those who would assume the vocation of a prophet to venture out from the fringes and to identify intimately with the struggles and plights of those we would constructively address.

PROCLAIMING HOPE WITH LOVE: FROM FALLEN CYNICS TO RISING PROPHETS

I think many Christian cynics may be fallen prophets. The prophet addresses God's people with engaged, sympathetic anguish, whereas the cynic ridicules God's people with distanced, apathetic annoyance. Perhaps God entrusted the latter with abrasive truths they dutifully shared, only to be cast so inhospitably to the fringes that they have yet to regain their footing.

Using the labels of "prophet" and "cynic" are convenient for heuristic purposes. Realistically, it is likely that we will find ourselves exhibiting characteristics of both when we embrace the task of offering reproof among God's people. It should be clear from the previous examples and passages that the biblical prophets at times displayed cynical symptoms in their ministries. Cynicism will always be a temptation and a potential vocational hazard for those enlisted in any form of prophetic criticism.

But when we come to understand that prophetic ministry is the outcry of God through feeble servants and occurs within the expansive narrative framework of God's redeeming work in the world, then we must assert that cynicism among prophets constitutes a departure from the vocational assignment.

To make the transition from the way of the cynic to the way of the prophet, it is necessary to embrace both *hopefulness* and *love*. Brueggemann emphasizes that the task of the prophet was not only to criticize but also to "energize."[6] Prophetic ministry must bear an eschatological direction—it must point the people of God to a hope beyond their power to materialize and even beyond their imaginations to grasp. This is not an unrealistic hope that Israel (or the church) will get it right—placing such hope in ourselves is an expression of idealism which, as we have seen (chap. 3), can be the quickest route into cynicism. The hope offered through the prophets was the hope that God himself would make all things right, that *God* would be the shepherd Israel's leaders failed to be (Ezekiel 34), that *God* would be the King no mortal son of David could be (Zechariah 14). And this hope is conjoined with a passionate love not only for God but also for the troubled people whom he intends to redeem.

DISCUSSION QUESTIONS

1. The author suggests that prophets had to balance a disgust with injustice alongside a love for unjust people. Has your own recognition of things amiss in the church been marked more by irritation or by heartache? Explain.

2. In what ways do our churches today need the prophetic voice?

3. How can the intentional distance created by the cynic actually damage the church *and* the cynic?

4. Have you noticed ways that the church pushes the prophetic voice to its fringes?

5. Does the idea of God expressing extreme emotions through his prophets disturb or comfort you? Have you ever felt as though God was allowing you to share in his "pathos"? If so, give an example.

the way
of the sage

Biblical Wisdom Instead of Cynical Intellectualism

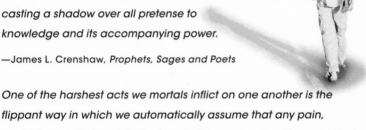

An incalculable factor permeates existence,
casting a shadow over all pretense to
knowledge and its accompanying power.

—James L. Crenshaw, *Prophets, Sages and Poets*

One of the harshest acts we mortals inflict on one another is the
flippant way in which we automatically assume that any pain,
anguish, or suffering visited upon another person must be a result of
that person's sins. Such unilinear thinking inflicts an unusual amount of
cruelty where it is often least deserved, and it only adds to the suffering
of the afflicted and their friends.

—Walter C. Kaiser Jr., *Grief and Pain in the Plan of God*

The words of the wise are like goads, and like nails firmly fixed are the
collected sayings; they are given by one Shepherd.

Ecclesiastes 12:11

How could this happen? Another question almost surfaces from their minds' darkest, most forbidden recesses (*if this has happened to him, could this happen to us?*), but the incompatibility of that question with their worldview renders it no more than a nagging mental ghost. The confounding reports of his misery had disrupted their busy schedules along with their minds. They are his friends, though, so there is nothing left to do but clear the calendar and make the journey to his estate.

As they near his property, something on the horizon catches their eye, something out of place. Something disorienting. A moving shape in the distance, writhing and contorted. The form is human. The behavior is alien. Whatever it may be, the faint image is out of place, dislodged from the sane order of life they are so fully invested in. The temptation is to give a wide berth. But there is an eerie familiarity to the figure on the dirt ahead of them. The closer they tread, the more gruesome becomes the sight through the haze of dust. When the moment of recognition occurs, it is too macabre to bear, too discomfiting to digest. All categories are rocked and then breeched. The sight before them seems unmoored from reality, beyond registry, so fantastical that all they can do is to fall in horror at the appalling spectacle before them, scraping its festering flesh with a jagged shard of clay. They collapse, weep, tear their expensive clothing, throw dust on their heads and say nothing for a week.

> And when they saw him from a distance, they did not recognize him. And they raised their voices and wept, and they tore their robes and sprinkled dust on their heads toward heaven. And they sat with him on the ground seven days and seven nights, and no one spoke a word to him, for they saw that his suffering was very great. (Job 2:12-13)

This is how Job's friends found him. Welcome to the wisdom literature.

THE SAGE IN ANCIENT ISRAEL

Kings were expected to maintain political stability, priests were to

maintain the religious institution and prophets provided abrasive protests against both in times of corruption. Less abrasive, though nonetheless subversive in their own ways, were sages, who subtly guided
matters of state in whispered counsels and critiqued Israelite pop culture with well-crafted writings.[1] Often referred to collectively in
Scripture as "the wise," some of these sages, like Hushai and
Ahithophel (2 Samuel 16–17), held high positions in royal courts.
Others were esteemed simply within the walls of their towns and villages, like the wise woman of Tekoa (2 Samuel 14) and the wise
woman of Abel (2 Samuel 20:16-22). These men and women were
honored for their wisdom, a treasure hailed as more precious than
silver, gold and jewels (Proverbs 8:10-11, 19; 16:16).

The Bible indicates that the celebration of wisdom began flourish-
ing with gusto during the reign of Solomon, the most famous of Israel's sages:

> And God gave Solomon wisdom and understanding beyond
> measure, and breadth of mind like the sand on the seashore, so
> that Solomon's wisdom surpassed the wisdom of all the people
> of the east and all the wisdom of Egypt. . . . He also spoke 3,000
> proverbs, and his songs were 1,005. He spoke of trees, from the
> cedar that is in Lebanon to the hyssop that grows out of the
> wall. He spoke also of beasts, and of birds, and of reptiles, and
> of fish. And people of all nations came to hear the wisdom of
> Solomon, and from all the kings of the earth, who had heard of
> his wisdom. (1 Kings 4:29-30, 32-34)

The tradition that developed with Solomon eventually produced
writings. Job, Proverbs and Ecclesiastes are the primary texts that
make up the biblical wisdom literature (the Song of Songs is sometimes included in this category, along with a number of psalms con-
taining wisdom themes).[2] This literature includes "practical wisdom"
expressed in reflective instructions or in pithy, memorable sayings (as
in Proverbs) and "speculative wisdom" expressed in biographical narratives and philosophical contemplations (as in Job and Ecclesiastes,

respectively).[3] Without the latter form of wisdom, the former can be naively streamlined into the trite formulas and empty platitudes we examined in the first half of this book.

Like the ancient sages, today's Christian cynics value insight and knowledge. Also in common with "the wise" in biblical Israel, contemporary cynics readily identify "folly" among God's people. But the sages' quest for knowledge was grounded in a worshipful reverence for God articulated as "the fear of the Lord." This foundation for wisdom is absent among many cynics.

It's not that we shouldn't bash sacred cows. It's not necessarily irreverent to deconstruct that which God himself deplores, and the sages certainly bashed some sacred cows in their own day. The problem is that cynical "wisdom" is often applied without a worshipful orientation or purpose. In addition, it is often applied with an elitist pleasure in scoffing at the ignorant masses. The critique of the sages behind the wisdom literature is marked by reverence for God and humility toward others (after all, "Pride goes before destruction, / and a haughty spirit before a fall" [Proverbs 16:18]).

For so many present-day Christian cynics, nothing is sacred. The sanctity and beauty of God's people and even God's own glory and honor are not above cynical critique. As discussed earlier in chapter six, cynics are often engaged in intellectual pursuits that end up challenging the accepted norms of Christian faith and doctrine. The insights and discoveries of such pursuits can lead to an elitist arrogance as young scholars grow boastful over the breadth of knowledge they possess in comparison to the wider membership of the church. What we find in the wisdom literature are approaches to correcting God's people, so prone to folly, that must override the way of the cynic or, as the sages may have put it, the way of the "scoffer."

THE BEGINNING OF WISDOM:
PROVERBS AND ARROGANT SCOFFING

I have just mentioned the title for someone whose prideful arrogance compels them to mock and deride others: " 'Scoffer' is the name of the

arrogant, haughty man / who acts with arrogant pride" (Proverbs
21:24). I think most of us would readily admit that this terse definition of a scoffer comports well with the stereotypical profile of a cynic.
The irony is that these scoffers, who confidently possess such knowledge that they have deemed themselves beyond need of correction
(Proverbs 9:7-8; 13:1; 15:12), are actually numbered not among "the
wise" but among the simple and the foolish: "How long, O simple
ones, will you love being simple? How long will scoffers delight in
their scoffing and fools hate knowledge?" (Proverbs 1:22).

The scoffer's pride sabotages his hopes for gaining insight, render-
ing his quest for knowledge ineffective: "A scoffer seeks wisdom in
vain, / but knowledge is easy for a man of understanding" (Proverbs
14:6). More is required than a bold willingness to swallow the bitter
pill of reality when it comes to pursuing wisdom. This pursuit can
only begin with a proper posture before God: "The fear of the LORD is
the beginning of wisdom" (Proverbs 9:10).[4]

This phrase "the fear of the LORD" opens and closes the first major
section of Proverbs (see Proverbs 1:7; 9:10), and it is found at the
book's closing (Proverbs 31:30), forming in both cases what in literary
terms is called an *inclusio*. This worshipful reverence cannot be
underestimated; without it, the cynic's pursuit of insight will be
doomed to failure from the start. Biblical wisdom is never divorced
from a humble and godly disposition—"He stores up sound wisdom
for the upright" (Proverbs 2:7, emphasis added). If we want to be numbered among the wise, then we must subordinate our academic ca-
reers, our late-night readings, our early morning studies and our sparring dialogues beneath the ultimate objective of fearfully honoring
the One who has no need for anyone's instructions. We might wield
cynical intellectualism and find respect from our interlocutors while
bantering about in the classroom, pub or coffee shop, but we will not
gain biblical wisdom until we submit ourselves humbly at God's feet.
(Besides, the insight so prized by cynical intellectuals may not be all
it's cracked up to be, as the author of Ecclesiastes seems to intimate
when he writes, "Of making many books there is no end, and much

study is a weariness of the flesh" [Ecclesiastes 12:12]!)

If we are to be entrusted with the task of teaching God's people and undeceiving them of pop Christianity, then we must devote ourselves to the pursuit of biblical wisdom, a pursuit that begins with honoring God. Without this humble posture we will become blind guides of the blind (Matthew 15:14; 23:16-26): "Whoever trusts in his own mind is a fool" (Proverbs 28:26); "Be not wise in your own eyes" (Proverbs 3:7).

LIVING WITH LEVIATHAN: JOB AND ANCIENT IDEALISM

As a literary form a biblical proverb is intended to concisely convey a general *principle*, not an automatic *promise*.[5] The sayings and aphorisms in the book of Proverbs were not to be mistakenly read as formulas that guaranteed wealth and success in life. Though Proverbs is thick with realism, there was the tendency in ancient popular culture to oversimplify the wisdom, presumptuously interpreting the sayings of the wise as sure promises rather than as guiding principles (nothing is new under the sun, is it?). Exploding against these formulaic and idealistic interpretations is the disturbing story about the wealthy man from the land of Uz: "Job is partly a reaction against a simplistic understanding of Proverbs."[6] It is an act of God's own infinite wisdom that he provided in our canon of Scripture not only this "practical wisdom" expressed in maxims and proverbs but also "speculative wisdom" that reminds us that life is too complex for a pithy slogan.

Job's story is the stuff that nightmares are made of: "the thing that I fear comes upon me, / and what I dread befalls me" (Job 3:25). We saw in the opening section of this chapter how Job's friends found him as a spectacle that demanded silence and horror. As the narrative unfolds it becomes clear that Job's friends had nothing more beneficial to offer him than the silence of that initial week. But in the face of *what should not be*, we feel compelled to protest, to provide a sensible explanation. So we open our mouths and begin rambling on about what God does not do. Would that those friends have remained mute: "miserable comforters are you all," Job tells them (Job 16:2).

Before I took the time in seminary to read through Job in one sitting, I esteemed the speeches of Eliphaz, Bildad and Zophar as sensible commentary on life's trials. After all, their remarks parallel nicely the language Christians regularly use today when offering consolation and comfort to others. Their theology is tidy, respectable, clear. But when we get to the end of the book, God rebukes them, because they "have not spoken of me what is right" (Job 42:7).

In his moment of greatest need Job is barraged with an idealizing misuse of wisdom that was as unsustainable in Uz as it is today. *Good things happen to good people, Job. God helps those who help themselves. God will never give you more than you can handle.* The popular wisdom that Job's story is written to silence is centered on ancient ideas regarding "retribution"—the righteous will experience blessing and the unrighteous misfortune.[7] If we live a clean life, then we won't get cancer and our business will thrive. If we *do* get cancer, if our business falters or if our marriage or ministry crumbles, then there must be unrighteousness somewhere in our lives. Each of Job's friends express this oversimplified, popular wisdom that bad things do not happen to good people who faithfully follow God.

Eliphaz:

> Remember: who that was innocent ever perished?
> Or where were the upright cut off? (Job 4:7)

Bildad:

> If you will seek God
>   and plead with the Almighty for mercy,
> if you are pure and upright,
>   surely then he will rouse himself for you
>   and restore your rightful habitation.
> And though your beginning was small,
>   your latter days will be very great. (Job 8:5-7)

Zophar:

> If iniquity is in your hand, put it far away,
>   and let not injustice dwell in your tents.

Surely then you will lift up your face without blemish;
> you will be secure and will not fear. (Job 11:14-15)

Job's friends were preaching idealized theology of the kind we addressed in chapter three. The god portrayed by this perspective is safely confined to certain parameters beyond which he cannot act. This is a theology that ever leans in our favor, a theology that posts certain "No Trespassing" signs that the pop god dutifully obeys.

Job's contrasting theology is offensive to his friends. Out of his misery he speaks of a God who has tromped across all the boundaries. Job's screeching laments are so theologically addling that his friends wish to clamp their hands over their ears, or more preferably over Job's mouth.

> Because their wisdom was radically threatened by Job, they could not be content with disagreement. They had to attack Job's whole position. This inevitably involved undermining the credibility of his cry. . . . [T]his is a classic move by ideologies that are challenged by the intensity of human sufferings: those who are suffering are feared, suspected, devalued, blamed.[8]

When the angry young fellow named Elihu decides he can no longer remain silent himself, his outbursts speak of a safe God who behaves himself in accordance with an unnuanced understanding of retribution:

> Therefore, hear me, you men of understanding:
> > far be it from God that he should do wickedness,
> > and from the Almighty that he should do wrong.
> For according to the work of a man he will repay him,
> > and according to his ways he will make it befall him.
> Of a truth, God will not do wickedly,
> > and the Almighty will not pervert justice. (Job 34:10-12)

In the face of unmanageable darkness, we are quick to explain what God *will not do*. But if you find yourself cursing the day of your birth, then contrary to the popular adage, God has probably given you more than you can handle (Job 3:1; cf. Jeremiah 15:10; 20:14-18).

The idealized theology that Job's story criticizes is premised on the human ambition to control life. And the kind of God Job worships and refuses to curse threatens all mortal aspirations to be in control. The uncomplicated god of Job's friends plays by the rules, blessing those who do good and afflicting only those who do wrong. This theology gives shape to a worldview in which human beings can control their fate. If they wish to succeed and become wealthy landowners, then they can practice righteousness, which will yield in formulaic simplicity the so-called good life. This theology is also reinforced by mystical experientialism: Eliphaz describes a visionary encounter with a spirit, a supernatural experience that in his view further legitimates his arguments (Job 4:12-21).

After so many unhelpful words, all voices finally fall silent in the story. Even Job's raucous pleas fade out to make way for the climactic speech that ends all speech. God speaks. And not from a sweet meadow or from a peaceful array of fluffy white clouds.

He speaks "out of the whirlwind" (Job 38:1). He speaks out of a tornado, out of a "natural" disaster.

The divine speeches that follow flatter no one but God himself. No satisfactory explanation is supplied for Job's suffering. God feels no obligation to show Job footprints in the sand. Instead of *theodicy*, God gives Job a *theophany:* "I have heard of you by the hearing of the ear, / but now my eye sees you" (Job 42:5). What God offers is an unsettling—yet exhilarating—glimpse of his glory. It is an unexpected approach to the ministry of consolation.

In his final words God speaks of two mythic beasts: Behemoth (Job 40:15-24) and Leviathan (Job 41:1-34). Some have interpreted these figures as the hippopotamus and the crocodile, respectively. The more likely explanation is that these are primordial beasts of the kind that appear as agents of chaos in ancient cosmogonies (creation accounts). In Genesis 1, God issues his powerful, creative speech against a viscous, mysterious darkness that many ancients would have understood as *chaos:* "the earth was without form and void, and darkness was over the face of the deep." In some ancient cosmogonies (which the readers of Job would have likely been familiar), great monsters would have been defeated along with the other powers of chaos by the creator god. However,

> in Job they are not defeated, and their cosmic menace and hostility to the human race are actually celebrated by [God]! Rather than destroying them to create an orderly world, Yahweh chooses to let them be (although on a leash). God tells Job that these monsters, the very symbols of evil, are alive and well, and that Job must live in the universe where they roam.[9]

I have told my children there are no such things as monsters. But maybe there are monsters. The mythic poetry of God's speech concerning the primordial beasts announces that we must share our existence with fierce, draconian forces beyond our power to control and subdue. Leviathan is out there.

Contrary to the aphoristic and vapid theology of Job's idealistic friends, God presents himself as one who defies all attempts at domestication, as one who knows no limits as defined by human convenience. The God of the book of Job is *free,* that is, free to act as he deems appropriate on the basis of a wisdom too profound for mortal minds.[10] And this divine freedom can sometimes seem to impinge on human existence. What does it do to our theology to know that Job's suffering can be traced back to a little wager God made with Satan in the opening chapters of Job? What does it do to our theology to know that God keeps a great, fire-breathing dragon as a pet?[11] This God we serve and worship keeps monsters as "playthings."[12]

God is so disappointed with Job's idealist friends by the end of the story that he will not even hear their prayers. They had misappropriated the kind of practical wisdom of the sort found in Proverbs to construct a shallow and safe vision of life. It would not be too far a stretch to suggest that there is also divine disappointment toward contemporary idealists who preach retribution, safeguarded by an uncomplicated God who always blesses the so-called righteous and never permits the wicked to flourish. The truth is that the wicked often *do* prosper, that sometimes Satan *is* granted permission to wreak havoc and that occasionally monstrous powers *are* heard braying and roaring in our ears. God is sovereign over all these characters and forces, but there is a complexity to the exercise of his sovereignty over them that will ever mystify and perplex us.

So we are justified in countering pop theology that twists the truth about God. But the cynics in the story are no more helpful than the idealists. Both Satan and Job's wife demonstrate hopelessness and cynical disengagement. Satan is skeptical of Job's righteousness, asserting that the man's nobility is only as deep as the goodness God has shown him. After God comments to Satan on Job's impressive piety, "Satan responds cynically by asking the thematic question of the book"[13]—"Does Job fear God for nothing?" (Job 1:9 NIV). Then Job's wife enters from the same side of the stage as Satan with her defeatist advice: "Curse God and die" (Job 2:9). Satan's skepticism is proven wrong, and the nihilism of Job's wife is instantly rebuked by Job himself as the wrong response to disillusionment: "You speak as one of the foolish women would speak. Shall we receive good from God, and shall we not receive evil?" (Job 2:10). So in Job's story we find a critique of both popular idealism and jaded cynicism.

If anyone has the right to remain a lifelong, card-carrying cynic in the story, it is Job—every character seems to let him down. But he does not eye his friends in contemptuous annoyance for long. Though God would not hear the idealists' prayers, we find in the final chapter that Job is instructed to intercede on their behalf. After all that pop theology, after all those rosy comments, Job prays for them. Would a cynic have prayed for mercy to be shown to his idealist friends?

THE VANITY OF LIFE: QOHOLETH AND *BIBLICAL* CYNICISM?

We now come to the third major work of biblical wisdom literature. The author of Ecclesiastes calls himself Qoholeth, a Hebrew term often translated as "Preacher." The presence of Ecclesiastes in the canon of Christian Scripture compels us to ask if there is such a thing as biblical cynicism.

Scholars are not quite sure what to make of Ecclesiastes. It seems that some would be comfortable labeling Qoholeth a cynic, while others would resist this designation by reminding readers that Ecclesiastes contains hopeful and positive comments along with the pessimistic and negative comments.[14] What Qoholeth's harsh words *do* make abundantly clear is that he is a vigorous realist who wrote to critique popular wisdom of his day:

> Time and time again one is driven to admit the truth of what Ecclesiastes has to say, even though one might not want to hear it. Here is the most real of the realists of the sacred writers. Here is the Hebrew writer least comfortable with conventional wisdom, and the most willing to challenge unexamined assumptions. No faith can survive long that is founded on the slippery slope of conceptually muddled piety, and in [Qoholeth], God has given us a tonic for our biblical faith.[15]

Christian cynics will likely be drawn to Qoholeth's tough realism. But does Ecclesiastes go beyond realism into a hopeless and disengaged cynicism? If this preacher were to preach next Sunday at our church, wouldn't the congregation consider him cynical?

In Ecclesiastes we have an *inclusio*. In the second verse of the book we read "Vanity of vanities, says the Preacher, vanity of vanities! All is vanity," and Qoholeth's words end in Ecclesiastes 12:8 with "Vanity of vanities, says the Preacher; all is vanity." Could there be a more cynical statement than "all is vanity"? Here are other remarks that have a cynical ring to them:

> I thought the dead who are already dead more fortunate than the living who are still alive. But better than both is he who has not yet been and has not seen the evil deeds that are done under the sun. (Ecclesiastes 4:2-3)

> It is better to go to the house of mourning
> than to go to the house of feasting. (Ecclesiastes 7:2)

He who digs a pit will fall into it,
> and a serpent will bite him who breaks through a wall.

He who quarries stones is hurt by them,
> and he who splits logs is endangered by them.

(Ecclesiastes 10:8-9)

Some might say that Ecclesiastes reads like a lengthy exposition of what we today call Murphy's Law. Qoholeth's honesty about his experience of life is absolutely brutal. He never offers touching promises or cheery platitudes ideal for plaques or coffee mugs. Cynical Christians may rejoice to find such an advocate of jaded disillusionment with life in the pages of their Bibles.

Qoholeth, however, defies being too easily crammed into the cynic's corner. Though bitingly satirical and undeniably skeptical, he does not write as one without joy or hope. He does not encourage apathy or a cynical withdrawal from the life of the broader community. His polemic against idealism is fierce, yet he encourages his readers to struggle to find joy and delight in the daily affairs of life, identifying God as the source of that joy and delight.

In chapter two I provided a brief autobiographical sketch of my personal journey from idealism to cynicism, and then of my ongoing attempt to embrace what I am calling hopeful realism. In the second chapter of Ecclesiastes, Qoholeth provides something very similar. He recounts an initial optimism that characterized his early adulthood: "I said in my heart, 'Come now, I will test you with pleasure; enjoy yourself' " (Ecclesiastes 2:1). This began a stage of his life in which he withheld no good thing from himself. With royal power and riches at his disposal, he constructed great buildings and gardens, lavished his table with fine food and drink, and indulged in the pleasures of female companionship. It was an energetic and well-resourced attempt at creating a personal experience of utopia.

This stage of his life, however, came crashing to an end with the disillusioning realization that all his projects and labors, all his grand explorations into pleasure amounted to a vain "striving after wind" (Ecclesiastes 2:11). This disillusionment seems to have precipitated a dark season of withdrawal in order to make sense of life: "So I turned to consider wisdom and madness and folly" (v. 12). His intellectual wrestling brought him to the point where he "hated life" (v. 17). Cynically aware that the fruit of all his labor and toil would be left to another upon his inevitable death, life became "grievous" (v. 17) to him, and he "gave up [his] heart to despair" (v. 20). This is someone who, with an unlimited arsenal of assets, devoted himself to philosophically examining and studying life. When the results of his exhaustive research were in, the assessment was that all of life is vain. His bubbles were burst, and no vestige of former idealism survived the disillusionment.

So far, those of us who struggle with cynicism can relate well to Qoholeth. We feel his disenchantment. We have some idea what it is like when reality violently interrupts a naively positive worldview. Some of us have given our hearts over "to despair." Nonetheless, a shift of perspective seems to transpire for Qoholeth, which many cynics never experience. At the end of chapter 2, after detailing his disillusioning discoveries, he concludes that human beings must embrace the simple delights of life that proceed from the generous (however mysterious) work of God's hand:

> There is nothing better for a person than that he should eat and drink and find enjoyment in his toil. This also, I saw, is from the hand of God, for apart from him who can eat or who can have enjoyment? (Ecclesiastes 2:24-25)

This theme of engaging in the affairs of life and finding simple joys even in the face of life's vicissitudes appears repeatedly throughout Ecclesiastes (see also Ecclesiastes 3:22; 6:1-6).

> I perceived that there is nothing better for them than to be joyful and to do good as long as they live; also that everyone should eat and drink and take pleasure in all his toil—this is God's gift to man. (Ecclesiastes 3:12-13)

> Behold, what I have seen to be good and fitting is to eat and drink and find enjoyment in all the toil with which one toils

under the sun the few days of his life that God has given him, for
this is his lot. Everyone also to whom God has given wealth and
possessions and power to enjoy them, and to accept his lot and
rejoice in his toil—this is the gift of God. For he will not much
remember the days of his life because God keeps him occupied
with joy in his heart. (Ecclesiastes 5:18-20)

Go, eat your bread in joy, and drink your wine with a merry
heart, for God has already approved what you do. Let your gar-
ments be always white. Let not oil be lacking on your head. Enjoy life with the wife whom you love, all the days of your vain
life that he has given you under the sun, because that is your
portion in life and in your toil at which you toil under the sun.
Whatever your hand finds to do, do it with your might, for there
is no work or thought or knowledge or wisdom in Sheol, to
which you are going. (Ecclesiastes 9:7-10)

Along with his positive encouragement to enjoy life and to appreciate divine gifts that appear along the way, Qoholeth promotes reverence
for God. Unlike Job, Qoholeth surprisingly brings no complaints before God, accepting his lot with hardened resolve.[16] Though life is futile
and toilsome, he does not blame God or justify anger toward him. Instead, he urges that we address God honorably and respectfully:

Guard your steps when you go to the house of God. To draw
near to listen is better than to offer the sacrifice of fools, for they
do not know that they are doing evil. Be not rash with your
mouth, nor let your heart be hasty to utter a word before God,
for God is in heaven and you are on earth. Therefore let your
words be few. (Ecclesiastes 5:1-2)

He also refers repeatedly to the fear of God, a theme we have already seen in Proverbs: "it will be well with those who fear God"
(Ecclesiastes 8:12; cf. Ecclesiastes 5:7; 7:18; 8:13). Ecclesiastes ends
with an epilogue, and the summation provided is that we must rever-
ently obey God: "The end of the matter; all has been heard. Fear God

and keep his commandments, for this is the whole duty of man" (Ecclesiastes 12:13).

In a brilliant work interfacing Ecclesiastes' wisdom with the claims of postmodernism, theologian Peter Leithart argues that Qoholeth (here "Solomon") teaches an eschatological perspective that embraces hopefulness. "Solomon's unblinking examination of power and oppression is pervaded by an eschatological faith that this world of tears under the sun is not the only world, a confidence that there is a time after the time under the sun."[17]

Leithart points out that Ecclesiastes ends with the expectation of divine judgment: "For God will bring every deed into judgment, with every secret thing, whether good or evil" (Ecclesiastes 12:14).[18] This is not a pessimistic statement but an expression of trust in the character of the mysterious God who will one day set straight the human frailty and the cosmic chaos that makes everything under the sun appear vain and senseless.

So, back to the questions at the opening of this section: Is Qoholeth a biblical cynic? Does Ecclesiastes provide an example of biblical cynicism? Others may reach different conclusions, but I would argue that Qoholeth is better labeled as a grim (though hopeful) realist than a bitter cynic. Is there really a difference? Yes. His exhortations to seek joy, his refusal to withdraw from life, his reverence for God and his hopeful orientation are not consistent with the cynicism so strong in the church today. As J. I. Packer indicates, it may even be possible that Ecclesiastes is an antidote to cynicism:

Among the seven deadly sins of medieval lore was sloth (acedia) —a state of hard-bitten, joyless apathy of spirit. There is a lot of it around today in Christian circles; the symptoms are personal spiritual inertia combined with a critical cynicism about the churches and a supercilious resentment of other Christians' initiative and enterprise.

Behind this morbid and deadening condition often lies the wounded pride of one who thought he knew all about the ways of God in providence and then was made to learn by bitter and bewildering experience that he didn't. This is what happens when we do not heed the message of Ecclesiastes.[19]

By listening to the realism of Qoholeth, our idealism might be dissolved so thoroughly that we would actually avoid being violently derailed and tossed into embittered cynicism.

Ecclesiastes does demonstrate, however, that at times we may be justified in resorting to harsh satire to express our frustrations with idealistic spirituality incompatible with the concrete inevitability of life's struggles. The author is writing to counteract popular misconceptions about life: "For Qoholeth, conventional wisdom was not only inadequate, but close to blasphemous"; "with burning eye and biting pen, Qoholeth challenged the overconfidence of the older wisdom and its misapplication in his culture."[20] In his critique of pop wisdom Qoholeth will at times quote popular clichés or proverbs and then refute them (which I also attempt to do in the first part of this book! See Ecclesiastes 2:14; 4:5; 9:18).[21]

Christians will be called to offer severe critiques of pop Christianity. But Qoholeth's example precludes full-blown cynicism. For those of us who would like to use impressive insight as a license to disengage from the broader community and rise above others in isolated (and pessimistic) enlightenment, we should hear Qoheleth calling us to enjoy even those seemingly mundane aspects of everyday life. We must hear him urging us to revere God regardless of our disillusionment. There is another lesson: we should forgo making brash statements about the apparent vanity of life until we have lived long enough and contemplated deep enough to do so. Christian cynics would do well to refrain from posting their caustic complaints in blogs and books until they have begun to apply their hearts to the search for wisdom as exhaustively as Qoholeth did before writing Ecclesiastes (a point I need to heed myself as I type these very words!).

BIBLICAL WISDOM VERSUS CYNICAL INTELLECTUALISM: SOME CONCLUDING WORDS FROM JAMES

Anyone can gain insight from their disillusionment, but wisdom is truly biblical only when it is grounded in "the fear of the Lord." The epistle of James is a New Testament example of Jewish wisdom literature, and early in the first pages we are taught that true wisdom is granted from God in response to childlike trust:

> If any of you lacks wisdom, let him ask God, who gives generously to all without reproach, and it will be given him. But let him ask in faith, with no doubting, for the one who doubts is like a wave of the sea that is driven and tossed by the wind. (James 1:5-6)

Later, James offers an important description of this biblical wisdom:

> But the wisdom from above is first pure, then peaceable, gentle, open to reason, full of mercy and good fruits, impartial and sincere. And a harvest of righteousness is sown in peace by those who make peace. (James 3:17-18)

"Pure," "peaceable," "full of mercy"—the contrast is sharp between this "wisdom from above" and the insight of jaded cynics, which is often arrogant, crass and hurtful. James would not discourage us from being subversive. He has a lot of harsh words to say about the pop cultural trends embraced by his readers! But the wisdom literature shows us that our intellectual and philosophical pursuits can only be utilized beneficially if they are sourced in a sincere desire to fearfully revere our all-wise God. An orientation toward eschatological hopefulness is less present in wisdom writings than in the prophets, but in placing such strong emphasis on reverence and worshipfulness, the ancient sages set the expectation that those who would embrace their style of teaching must be grounded firmly in a love for God.

As he has always done, God is raising up servants to instruct and even chasten his people. If we wish to be enlisted in this mission in the way of the biblical sage, then we will need to be reverent along with being subversive, humble along with being shrewd. The friction between Job and his idealistic friends was strong, but we have seen how he ended up praying for them. Where are the cynics at the end of the story? Satan and Job's wife are nowhere to be found. The idealists are restored in friendship to Job but the cynics fade away into obscurity. Again as Qoholeth would remind us, "there is nothing new under the sun" (Ecclesiastes 1:9); the cynics are still destined to fade out of the picture. So follow the way of the sage, not the cynic.

DISCUSSION QUESTIONS

1. Who has played the role of a sage or wise counselor in your life? Describe his or her ministry to you.

2. Name some ways that the wisdom of this world differs from the wisdom of God's kingdom. Which type of wisdom do you most often see displayed in our churches?

3. Has there been a time in your life when you misapplied biblical wisdom? Explain.

4. If the "beginning of wisdom is the fear of the Lord," name one or two ways you will set yourself to the task of becoming biblically wise.

5. In moments of despair, how have you offered or received comfort that was simply unhelpful (and perhaps even painful)?

10 the way of the tragic poet

Worshipful Lament Instead of Cynical Complaint

How long, O Lord?
—throughout the Psalms

[The Psalter] has this peculiar marvel of its own, that within it are represented and portrayed in all their great variety the movements of the human soul.

—Athanasius, Letter to Marcellinus on the Interpretation of the Psalms

The psalms of negativity, the complaints of various kinds, the cries for vengeance and profound penitence are foundational to a life of faith in this particular God. Much Christian piety is romantic and unreal in its positiveness. As children of the Enlightenment, we have censored and selected around the voice of darkness and disorientation, seeking to go from strength to strength, from victory to victory. But such a way not only ignores the Psalms; it is a lie in terms of our experience. . . . The Jewish reality of exile, the Christian confession of crucifixion and cross, the honest recognition that there is an untamed darkness in our life that must be embraced—all of this is fundamental to the gift of new life.

—Walter Brueggemann, Spirituality of the Psalms

O daughter of my people, put on sackcloth,
  and roll in ashes;
make mourning as for an only son,
  most bitter lamentation,
for suddenly the destroyer
  will come upon us.

Jeremiah 6:26

In chapters eight and nine we have seen how the Old Testament prophets and sages confronted populist religious trends. The prophets were called to participate in the stormy conflux within God's heart of both rage and compassion toward Israel and Judah. The sages were called to wrestle with things that could never be known about God's mind and ways. At moments in both the prophetic and wisdom literature, we can detect the authors' raw pain of disillusionment with God's people.

But what if our disillusionment is not so much with God's people but with *God himself?* What if our enemy seems to be the one on whom we most confidently rely? Our Sunday school class will fail us. Our pastors will fail us. Our spouses, children, siblings and parents will fail us. At times it will appear as though *God* has failed us. Where will we go when we've turned to him who is the first and the last, the beginning and the end, and he is either nowhere to be found or, even worse, the one who seems to be the source of our affliction?

Though the cynicism of most Christians today seems more directed toward other Christians and to the institutional identity of the church, our cynicism is often found in deeper veins and in darker places in our hearts and minds—if we are honest, many of us are cynical toward God. We tend to be less talkative about our disillusionment with him than we are about our disillusionment with the church or Christianity in general. This is due in part to a degree of apprehension instilled within us regarding the numinous. It is also due to the fact that we lack language to talk about it.

For vocabulary and grammar suitable to such dark and bitter pain, we turn to the despondent laments of tragic poets who, before us, suffered from disillusionment with God. Though most of these haunting cries are found in the Psalms, we have already encountered some cries of the poets—the prophet Jeremiah and the sage behind the book of Job were certainly familiar with the Hebrew language of lament. When we find ourselves in spiritual shambles, quaking in our disappointment with God, these tragic poets and their tumultuous words help us navigate our way through the murky waters.

The Hebrew title for the book of Psalms is *těhillîm*, which means "Praises."[1] Scholars have identified various categories of our 150 psalms, and the largest of these categories is the *lament*, representing roughly a third of the entire Psalter. So within the worship book of Israel, within the pages of that collection designated as "Praises," there is *mourning*. There is *pain*. There is *groping* in the dark. We find rejoicing and triumphant singing in Psalms, but we also find the dissonant groaning of those who are disenfranchised, not just with their community of faith but with the God who is the object of their faith.

Why, O LORD, do you stand far away?
Why do you hide yourself in times of trouble? (Psalm 10:1)

I say to God, my rock:
    "Why have you forgotten me?" (Psalm 42:9)

I suffer your terrors. (Psalm 88:15)

You have taken me up and thrown me down. (Psalm 102:10)

We are not supposed to talk like this in church on Sunday mornings, are we? The crying pleas of the lament psalms sound like banned
language to our ears, the kind of seditious talk that would get us into
trouble if anyone ever heard it coming from our lips. The sentiments,
however, are not alien to us. Though rarely voiced publicly, they lie
unsurfaced within our troubled hearts and minds during certain seasons of our lives.

We seem to think that praising God involves singing joyful songs
as "shiny happy people."[2] Many of our churches incorporate the brief
"meet and greet" time in the Sunday morning service, during which it
is quite awkward to respond to "How are you?" with something other
than "Fine." (Few of us feel free to be *not* fine at church!) Worship
pastors may coach the choir or praise team to maintain a vibrant smile
during the songs, but anyone who has ever led worship on Sunday
morning knows how difficult it is to rouse a sleepy congregation into
enthusiastic singing when they are beset with mortgage payments,
nagging family issues and interpersonal conflicts—no matter how
wide the smile on the faces of backup vocalists.

It is understandable and noble to regard our time at church as a
happy, peaceful place of refuge. But no refugee camp provides healthy
refuge by denying the reality of whatever calamity dislodged its resi-
dents from their normal affairs.

The lament psalms show us that tragic poetry is as valid a part of
our worship as joyful choruses. Proclaiming our grief and misery before God can be just as worshipful as singing of the relief and delight
we experience from his deliverance and salvation. To exclude lament
is to join hands with our misguided culture "which wants to deny and
cover over the darkness we are called to enter."[3] Claus Westermann,
one of the most influential scholars on the psalms in the twentieth
century, writes that "it is an illusion to suppose or to postulate that
there could be a relationship with God in which there was only praise
and never lamentation. . . . [S]omething must be amiss if praise of
God has a place in Christian worship but lamentation does not.[4]

The cries and blunt questions directed to God in the Psalms, however, are only appropriate within the context of *worship*. The voluminous presence of laments in the Psalter shows us that just as our responses to victory and divine deliverance must be acts of faithful devotion, so also our expressions of pain and misery before God must be acts of faithful devotion, however discordant the tone.

At some point along the way the Western church stopped associating weeping with worship. It probably occurred about the time we stopped reading and preaching so much from Lamentations and those more ominous psalms.[5] We may rejoice to see a few tears in response to a moving song or message (see chap. 5), but we seem unable to truly value the regular expression of sorrow as a necessary dimension to our worship. Because of this, we have become less hospitable to the dispirited and injured individuals for whom the church should serve as a haven for healing. When the depressed and the disconsolate are in our midst, do they feel free *not* to answer "fine, just fine" to our greetings? Are they silently shunned when they talk of God as though he is their oppressor rather than their Deliverer? Does the worship service provide them with a context in which they are encouraged to express their *pain* (and not just their *joy*) as an act of worshiping God? What are the beleaguered and downcast to do when they find themselves in need of singing to God with sad songs in minor keys if all that is provided are joyful refrains in major keys?

When the church fails to provide some outlet for crying to God from "out of the depths" (Psalm 130:1), then broken souls will turn elsewhere. To our shame the bar stool and the psychiatrist's couch are often viewed as more hospitable contexts for tormented souls than the chapel's pew. By minimizing—or worse, eliminating—the biblical role of lament in the life of the church, we are communicating to the world, as well as to members of our own congregations, that they must take their struggles with God elsewhere. Brokenness turns into bitterness when God is denied access to our wounds and when pain is removed from the context of worship. The absence of lament on Sunday mornings is therefore promoting cynicism. So once again, we find the church unintentionally culpable for populating our own ranks with cynics.

WORSHIPING IN A MINOR KEY: LITERARY AND THEOLOGICAL FEATURES IN THE LAMENTS

Bill Mallonee, a brilliant songwriter unafraid to write from "out of the depths," refers to "love songs in the minor key" in one of his many troubled (yet beautiful) ballads.[6] Love involves such poignant moments of despair and struggle that, at times, only a minor key will suffice. The same is true when it comes to our relationship with God. We do not have the sheet music that many of the psalms were played or sung to, but I have a hard time believing that some ancient Israelite ever sang "My tears have been my food / day and night" (Psalm 42:3) in the key of C major.

The biblical laments testify to the comforting reality that we do not have to put on a pretty façade in order to appear before God. We can address him in our most panicked moments of disarray and confusion. This raw, crushing pain of a soul estranged from God can be so severe that to express it demands making appeal to a higher form of language—poetry is required. Appearing in multiple places throughout the Old Testament beyond the psalms, these sad songs and poems constitute a recognizable literary genre.[7]

Biblical laments exhibit a couple of literary features that bear tremendous theological importance for *how* we address God out of darkness and despair. The first is that most lament psalms begin with an immediate address to God, usually employing the covenant name Yahweh (denoted in our English translations in small caps as "LORD" or "GOD").[8] This is no minor detail in the structure of laments—such an initial invocation demonstrates that *God* is ultimately the one to whom we turn, even when he seems to be the reason behind our pain. This God-ward orientation places the complaint within the context of worship: "The lament is not a mere venting of emotion intended primarily to provide emotional relief to the psalmist; rather it is a supplication for divine assistance, and in this it is an implicit statement of faith."[9]

The fact that laments regularly open with "O Yahweh/LORD" confirms that our *suffering* is to be incorporated into our *worship*. If pain and disillusionment are removed from the realm of personal communication with God, then further bitterness is inevitable. In exposing their wounds to Yahweh, the stricken poets were presenting themselves before a personal God who had entered into a sacred covenant with his people.

The direct divine address of the lament psalms encourages us to approach God in our own anguish, though we must do so as worshipers who have such a personal relationship with him that we can call him by his revealed covenant name. Eugene Peterson observes of the psalms: "Every skeptical thought, every disappointing venture, every pain, every despair that we can face *is lived through and integrated into a personal, saving relationship with God.*"[10] Similarly, Brevard Childs notes: "The Psalms reflect the most concrete human experiences possible, *but always in relation to the object of its praise and complaint, who is God.*"[11]

The opening address of God in the psalms of lament demonstrates that, in spite of the emotional turmoil of their tortured speeches, these tragic poets were vigorously God-centered. We must therefore bring our disillusionment *with* God *to* God, and this address is worshipful in that it acknowledges God as the one audience who matters most:

O Lord, all my longing is before you;
my sighing is not hidden from you. (Psalm 38:9)

But as for me, my prayer is to you, O LORD. (Psalm 69:13)

A second literary feature of the lament psalms instructive for how we deal with our disillusionment with God is the sudden insertion of praise or expressions of hope in the midst of the despairing pleas. Almost every lament psalm has at least some inkling of hopefulness. In many cases, the shift from complaint to praise is found at the end of the psalm. This "internal transition" is so common that Westermann is convinced that "there is not a single Psalm of lament that stops with lamentation. Lamentation has no meaning in and of itself."[12] Psalm 13 is often cited as an example that epitomizes the standard literary structure of the lament psalm. Notice not only the im-

mediate address to Yahweh but also the transition from agonizing to
praising in the conclusion (indicated by italics)—

> How long, O LORD? Will you forget me forever?
>   How long will you hide your face from me?
> How long must I take counsel in my soul
>   and have sorrow in my heart all the day?
> How long shall my enemy be exalted over me?

> Consider and answer me, O LORD my God;
>   light up my eyes, lest I sleep the sleep of death,
> lest my enemy say, "I have prevailed over him,"
>   lest my foes rejoice because I am shaken.

> *But I have trusted in your steadfast love;*
>   *my heart shall rejoice in your salvation.*
> *I will sing to the LORD,*
>   *because he has dealt bountifully with me.*

This internal transition is so common that it seems to be a widely
accepted feature for the genre of lament poetry (for other clear examples, see Psalms 3; 6; 10–14; 17; 22; 28; 32; 41, 43; 53–55; 60; 62; 64; 69;
73; 75; 85; 94; 109; 130; 140–143). The poets could creatively alter this
standard format by bracketing the lamenting prayer with bold profes-
sions of confidence (e.g., Psalm 27), by placing a brief expression of
praise or hope in the middle of the psalm before resuming the lament
(e.g., Psalm 38), or by stating that God has heard the prayers at the very
beginning before actually voicing the lament (e.g., Psalm 120).

These regular expressions of hope and praise in the psalms of lament show us that we need not "grieve as others do who have no
hope" (as Paul would write much later to grieving Christians [1 Thessalonians 4:13]). The sudden mood swings from agony to confidence
in the laments attest to a propitious perspective in which suffering
and sorrow are only temporary conditions that will one day give way
to eventual rescue.

With these two literary features—the immediate address of God and the transition from sorrow to hope—the tragic poets of Israel encourage us to bring our pain and grief before the God who will one day set us free. Disillusionment with God does not license us to cease worshiping him. When we cannot worship in a major key with the joyful blasts of trumpets as in Psalm 150, then we worship in a minor key as in Psalm 22 by turning to him even when it takes the last shred of strength in our wearied bones.

CAN WE QUESTION GOD OR BE ANGRY WITH HIM?

By pointing out the opening address to Yahweh and those concluding shifts from despair to praise, I do not mean to dismiss the brutal and harsh words found in between. Contained within the psalms of lament are brazen questions posed to God. Do the poems of lament in Scripture give us permission to angrily question God?

In the previous sections we have already encountered passages in which tragic poets pose to God hard questions. In Psalm 13 alone the hurtful inquiry "How long?" occurs four times in the first two verses! There are plenty of other examples throughout the Psalter:

My God, my God, why have you forsaken me?
Why are you so far from saving me, from the words of my
    groaning? (Psalm 22:1)

Why have you forgotten me? (Psalm 42:9)

Why do you cast us off forever? (Psalm 74:1)

Why should the nations say,
    "Where is their God?" (Psalm 79:10; cf. Psalm 115:2)

Will you be angry with us forever?
    Will you prolong your anger to all generations?
Will you not revive us again,
    that your people may rejoice in you? (Psalm 85:5-6)

O LORD, how long shall the wicked,
    how long shall the wicked exult? (Psalm 94:3)

If you were in a prayer meeting and overheard someone addressing God in this way, you might subtly create a bit of space between the two of you in case of a sudden lightning strike. Such a sullen disposition before God seems daring and brazen. Is it really okay to bring such questions before the throne of the almighty God? Listen to these appalling questions the author of Lamentations writes about the Babylonian siege of Jerusalem:

> Look, O LORD, and see!
>> With whom have you dealt thus?
> Should women eat the fruit of their womb,
>> the children of their tender care?
> Should priest and prophet be killed
>> in the sanctuary of the Lord? (Lamentations 2:20)

Can we really subject God to this kind of accusatory questioning?

In some cases it may be helpful to distinguish between questioning God and asking God questions. The difference between the two is found in the acknowledgment of where we stand before him. No matter how fierce the trial, no matter how severe the torment, we are always the *supplicant*. We are never in the position to demand mastery over our fate. We are always clay in the hand of the Potter. But we *can* ask questions of God, even pointed, impassioned, tear-choked and agonizing questions. In each of the psalms just cited, the questions are eventually followed by the characteristic transition from despair to hope or praise. The tragic poet of Lamentations even manages to break out into energetic praise in the middle of chapter 3. So though we may bring our aching, yearning questions before God, we do so as worshipers who are ever pressing toward praise, rejoicing that "the reason the darkness can be faced and lived in is that even in the darkness, there is One to address."[13]

The biblical laments affirm at the very least that we can ask God hard questions. But can we actually question him as angry interrogators? When we are longing for justice, are we ever justified in bulleting accusatory questions heavenward?

There are not only painful questions thrown out to God in the lament psalms, but assertions (accusations?) that God is to blame for the suffering:

Your arrows have sunk into me,
    and your hand has come down on me. (Psalm 38:2)

I am spent by the hostility of your hand. (Psalm 39:10)

All your breakers and your waves
    have gone over me. (Psalm 42:7)

You have made the land to quake; you have torn it open.
    (Psalm 60:2)

You have put me in the depths of the pit,
    in the regions dark and deep. (Psalm 88:6)

Such accusations appear in frenzied succession in certain sections of Lamentations:

He has driven and brought me
    into darkness. . . .
He has made my flesh and my skin waste away;
    he has broken my bones. . . .
He has made me dwell in darkness. . . .
    he has made my chains heavy; . . .
    he shuts out my prayer. . . .
He turned aside my steps and tore me to pieces;
    he has made me desolate. . . .
He drove into my kidneys
    the arrows of his quiver. . . .
He has made my teeth grind on gravel. (Lamentations 3:2, 4,
        6-8, 11, 13, 16)

This type of language might make us uncomfortable. Except, of course, when we find God's arrows sticking out of our own hearts, when we feel the weight of his hand smashing *us* into the dark pit.

Then the language is comforting because we realize that others have suffered before us. Thomas Merton wrote that "there is no night of the soul that has not been experienced before us by the psalmists."[14] But do these questions and accusations give us freedom to arraign God to our own courts and throttle him for answers?

Before we serve God a subpoena and summon his presence to hear our case, it would be wise to consider how God might respond. In chapter nine we glimpsed one of the few places in the Bible where we have a record of God's reply to prayers of lament. In his pleas and demands for justice, Job used courtroom language, hurling questions to a silent deity who seemed asleep at the wheel of the universe. But when God broke his silence, it was not with apologies or explanations. God responded to Job's long list of questions with a litany of his own questions:

> Then the LORD answered Job out of the whirlwind and said:
>
> "Who is this that darkens counsel by words without knowledge? Dress for action like a man;
>   *I will question you*, and you make it known to me.
> "Where were you when I laid the foundation of the earth?
>   Tell me, if you have understanding.
> Who determined its measurements—surely you know!
>   Or who stretched the line upon it?
> (Job 38:1-5, emphasis added)

God continues to barrage Job with questions, the most penetrating seems to be this one:

> Shall a faultfinder contend with the Almighty?
> He who argues with God, let him answer it. (Job 40:2)

Job had sought to place God on the witness stand for interrogation, but the roles were abruptly reversed. Know this: *questioning God may result in God questioning us*.[15] Just be prepared for the tables to be turned.

But if a tragic poet can pen something like "Awake! Why are you sleeping, O Lord?" (Psalm 44:23), implying that God is sleeping on the job and commanding that he finally roll out of his comfy bed, then surely we should feel free to address him in our pained fury, right? In his recent book *The Sacredness of Questioning Everything*, David Dark reflects on the lament language in Scripture: "When I consider the prayer-speech preserved in the psalms, the lamentations, and the cries of the prophets, I'm reminded that the biblical witness does not summon us to censor ourselves in prayer."[16] Richard Foster shares similar sentiments when he writes that the lament psalms "give us permission to shake our fist at God one moment and break into doxology the next."[17]

Before we rush the throne of God with raised fists and raised voices, though, we should consider, along with God's response to Job, those strong warnings in Scripture against approaching God haphazardly or arrogantly (which would surely apply even if we do eventually intend to break out into doxology):

> Woe to him who quarrels with his Maker,
>   to him who is but a potsherd among the potsherds on the
>   ground.
> Does the clay say to the potter,
>   "What are you making?"
> Does your work say,
>   "He has no hands?" . . .
>
> They will say of me, "In the LORD alone
>   are righteousness and strength."
> All who have raged against him
>   will come to him and be put to shame. (Isaiah 45:9, 24 NIV)

Echoing these sentiments, Paul writes,

> You will say to me then, "Why does he still find fault? For who can resist his will?" But who are you, O man, to answer back to God? Will what is molded say to its molder, "Why have you made me like this?" (Romans 9:19-20)

So, in light of Job's experience and these warnings, *may we angrily question God?*

No. Well, at least I don't think so (but maybe). The vagueness of my answer to our hard question is intentional.

Whether it is right or not to angrily question God, the reality impressed on us as we read the biblical laments is that at times we *will* angrily question God. Somewhere in the tension between "woe to him who quarrels with his Maker" and "Awake! Why are you sleeping, O Lord?" we must acknowledge that God graciously permits limited space for us to vent our languishing, bitter pain in anger. I don't think God *welcomes* or *encourages* our indignant interrogations—I'm just saying he seems to graciously provide a bit of room for them, and he is big enough to handle the fuss. Though Job's questions were ultimately drowned out by God's own questions back to him, it was Job's friends—the ones who tried to shut him up—who God reprimanded for speaking about him wrongly.

I would never recommend the raising of fists or angry voices to heaven. Never. Even so, I would never want to deny or ignore the gnawing darkness of Psalm 88, one of the rare lament psalms in which there is no discernible transition out of despair. Those terrible, weary words, so pregnant with aching, groaning misery, are ever-screeching and shouting out from the dead center of our Bibles. So there may indeed be some mysterious place between blasphemy and reverence from which we may cry out to God in utter horror and in bitter anger. Should we ever find ourselves in such a precarious, risky place, however, we must remember in our importunate banging on heaven's door that "all who have raged against him / will come to him and be put to shame" (Isaiah 45:24 NIV; cf. 2 Kings 19:28; Isaiah 37:29). We will likely find ourselves humbled and silenced like Job, but perhaps in such catastrophic pain it is possible that no other path is available.

May God help us—and forgive us.

IMPRECATORY PSALMS: "O THAT YOU WOULD SLAY THE WICKED" (REALLY?)

Along with the questions and accusations, another messy feature of the lament psalms is the common appearance of prayers for vengeance. Our disillusionment with God often arises because we feel that he is unconcerned with the abuse we endure at the hands of others. Whether it is his decision to allow cliché Christianity to thrive so unchecked in our churches or his refusal to intervene when we are being victimized in some way, we often become cynics when it seems as though God has failed to mete out justice ("How long, O Lord, will you look on?" [Psalm 35:17]). The tragic poets of Israel felt somewhat free (perhaps even *obligated*) to voice demands for vindication in their laments. Is this okay for us to do today?

When I first read Psalm 139 in college, I decided to set it to music. If found that the words flowed so elegantly in the cheery and majestic key of C major. Except for the words found near the end of the psalm:

> Oh that you would slay the wicked, O God!
>> O men of blood, depart from me!
> They speak against you with malicious intent;
>> your enemies take your name in vain!
> Do I not hate those who hate you, O LORD?
>> And do I not loathe those who rise up against you?
> I hate them with complete hatred;
>> I count them my enemies. (Psalm 139:19-22)

I have to admit that these verses didn't make the cut for my little song. Sure, I felt uncomfortable about selectively censoring Scripture like that, but that was not quite as uncomfortable as trying to sing hate-filled curses from my piano bench.

Such imprecations against the enemies of God appear throughout the psalms, especially (and unsurprisingly) in the psalms of lament.[18]

> Let their way be dark and slippery,
>> with the angel of the LORD pursuing them! (Psalm 35:6)

> Let them be like the snail that dissolves into slime,
>> like the stillborn child who never sees the sun. (Psalm 58:8)

> Let them be blotted out of the book of the living;
>> let them not be enrolled among the righteous. (Psalm 69:28)

May his children wander about and beg,
    seeking food far from the ruins they inhabit! (Psalm 109:10)

And according to Old Testament scholar John Goldingay, the most
offensive passage in the Psalter:

O daughter of Babylon, doomed to be destroyed,
    blessed shall he be who repays you
    with what you have done to us!
Blessed shall he be who takes your little ones
and dashes them against the rock! (Psalm 137:8-9)[19]

It is hard to imagine that there could ever be a time when the faithful could pray such prayers in their disillusionment over God's (apparent) neglect of justice. As we must hold the tragic poets' questioning
of God in tension with other biblical passages, we must read these
imprecations in tension with New Testament teachings that provide a
different framework for approaching enemies (see chap. 11). Does this
mean, however, that there is never a time when we can pray for God
to bring divine vengeance?

Less than a year ago I read an article in a Christian magazine about
a militia leader who haunted the rough terrain in a politically con-
tested region of central Africa. His marauding band of fellow soldiers
would suddenly explode out of the jungle like wild beasts, shooting
startled villagers and burning their homes. They raped women and
little girls. They dismembered children. The leader of this paramili-
tary group could not be stopped, and there seemed to be no limits to
the depravity. I read how they once force-fed a mother the unborn
child they had just sliced out of her belly.

I found myself instantly praying for divine vengeance.

I prayed hard. I was infuriated with this militia leader and appalled
that God was allowing his rampages to continue unabated.

I did ask that mercy would be shown to him, but I also prayed for
a definitive end to his violent campaigns. I did not feel comfortable
uttering those words. I am not sure if I should have prayed what I
prayed. What I do know is that a month later, while reading an inter-

national news journal, I saw that this militia leader had been captured and arrested. Other Christians must have been on their knees as well. "With my mouth I will give great thanks to the LORD; / . . . for he stands at the right hand of the needy" (Psalm 109:30-31).

It is easy to dismiss the tragic poets' curses on their foes as the barbaric language of an ancient, warmongering culture. Such prayers can be so distasteful when we read them while sipping lattes in quaint cafés or while comfortably ensconced on the leather sofa before the soft glow of our gas fireplace. But we need to learn to read the imprecatory prayers in the lament poems as the cries of men, women and children who lift their eyes to see wild-eyed terrorists racing out of the jungle and into their villages. These desperate pleas "give voice to the oppressed and voiceless. To remove these psalms from our liturgy is to conspire with oppressors and silence those whose lives are swallowed up by powerful adversaries."[20]

These imprecations help us to pray with the poor and subjugated— Psalm 10 must be such a helpful lament for those who work with refugees, abandoned children and victims of the sex trade. And those of us who live free from the fear of raiding militia groups and the unending anxiety of grinding poverty are never entirely safe from catastrophic abuse. The imprecatory prayers enable us to appear before God as roughed up and messed up victims of immorality and crime: "It is an act of profound faith to entrust one's most precious hatreds to God, knowing they will be taken seriously."[21]

Imprecatory laments, however, must not be employed for self-centered means. The prayers for vindication are overwhelmingly *God-centered*, just as we have seen that the complaints of the Psalter are ultimately God-centered. We must remember that these furious cries for justice in the lament psalms are still a part of Israel's hymn book— the ultimate purpose of the prayers for judgment is the worship of the Judge. It would be all too easy for jaded Christians to wrongly appeal to the tragic poets' demands for vengeance to justify personal vendettas with others or grudges toward the church. The imprecations of the psalms and lament, however, are the indignant protests of those who

have been trained in the righteousness of Yahweh and refuse to toler-
ate injustice. Though the experience of their enemies' assaults is
acutely personal, their desire for personal vindication is ultimately
rooted in their desire for *divine* vindication. It is *God's* honor that is
most at stake when the wicked prosper and cruel assailants take what
they want.[22]

> For the sin of their mouths, the words of their lips,
>   let them be trapped in their pride.
> For the cursing and lies that they utter,
>   consume them in wrath;
>   consume them till they are no more,
> that they may know that God rules over Jacob
>   to the ends of the earth. (Psalm 59:12-13)

> Fill their faces with shame,
>   that they may seek your name, O LORD.
> Let them be put to shame and dismayed forever;
>   let them perish in disgrace,
> that they may know that you alone,
>   whose name is the LORD,
> are the Most High over all the earth. (Psalm 83:16-18)

> But you, O GOD my Lord,
>   deal on my behalf for your name's sake. (Psalm 109:21)

The curses in the laments are as theological as they are personal,
because the tragic poets are operating out of the hopeful conviction
that God will one day judge the corruption and oppression in our
world and create some new situation in which righteousness abounds.
Though the New Testament recasts how we treat our enemies as we
await this new situation, we may still pray passionately for immediate
justice as we anticipate the eventual day of judgment. The imprecatory section of Psalm 69 is cited by both Paul and Luke in the New
Testament (Romans 11:9-10; Acts 1:20) and the martyrs in John's
apocalyptic vision cry out "in a loud voice" words that seem more fit-

ting in an Old Testament lamentation: "O Sovereign Lord, holy and true, how long before you will judge and avenge our blood on those who dwell on the earth?" (Revelation 6:10).

These hostile prayers of the tragic poets will disturb the comfortable. For those who are disillusioned with God because they have suffered violently at the hands of others, they may provide comfort; though their presence in Scripture must not be used as excuses for nurturing a begrudging, self-centered bitterness. They instead challenge injured cynics to ground their hope for justice in the righteousness of God and not in their own sense of self-dignity.

WORSHIPFUL LAMENT VERSUS CYNICAL COMPLAINT

We have been working through some of the most shocking words found in our Bibles. In the midst of all the anger and frustration directed both to God and to others in these Old Testament laments, we now ask, is it possible to draw a distinction between *cynical* complaining and *biblical* complaining?

Cynical Christians may find no closer companions in Scripture than the tragic poets, who dared to express their disillusionment *with* God *to* God. They may be pleasantly startled to find their own cries and protests echoed in the biblical laments. For complaints to be truly biblical, however, they must ultimately be characterized by *worship*. Now, as discussed earlier, worship can be in the form of weeping—it does not have to appear tidy and nice. Worship can even be in the form of posing questions to God since, in the questioning, there is the implicit acknowledgment that God is the one with the final say. Worship does not have to be in C major. But any attempt to approach God outside of worship is not only wrong, but dangerous (and in the end, impossible, actually). Even dreary Psalm 88 begins with the characteristic address of God by his covenant name Yahweh, indicating a God-ward orientation on behalf of the beleaguered poet. So the ultimate distinction between worshipful lament and cynical complaint is the orientation of worship.

Another distinction is that worshipful lament strives toward hope-

fulness and joyful praise. Though in very rare instances the tragic poets do not quite make the transition, in the overwhelming majority of
the laments they cannot help but interrupt or even conclude their
mourning with acclamations of praise and assertions of confidence in
God's eventual deliverance.[23] The literary format of the biblical lament theologically pressures us to be ever moving away from gloom
into hopefulness. There will be rare moments, perhaps, when our
wounds are so severe that we cannot make the transition, but we will
become further embittered as cynics if we do not somehow strive with
whatever tattered shreds of hope are left to bring our disillusionment
to a joyous end.

We have seen repeatedly that the orientation toward worship and
the attempt to transition from despair to joy are the two elements most
characteristic of biblical laments. If these two elements are missing,
then our complaints can only be labeled as cynical. Mocking irreverence and the absence of hope are classic elements of cynicism. The
tragic poets no doubt wrestled with cynical feelings, but we find in
their bleak artistry the inclination to drag their bruised souls and sick
bodies to the feet of their covenant-keeping God and to stumble somehow in the dark toward even the tiniest cracks of distant daylight.

The brokenness of human misery before God may recede into bitterness, but healing comes when we bring our maladies to him and
check into his healing ward. We do this not by avoiding him in disillusionment but by crying out *to him* from the depths and striving with
all our might to grasp onto something hopeful from his hand. There
may be no greater act of worship than an embittered cynic daring to
bring his injured, angry soul before the presence of the One who
seems to have caused the injuries.

Let the bones that you have broken rejoice. (Psalm 51:8)

Why are you cast down, O my soul,
    and why are you in turmoil within me?
Hope in God; for I shall again praise him,
    my salvation and my God. (Psalm 42:11)

The imprecations and torrential questions demand that we make another point in distinguishing between biblical complaints and cynical complaints: *the struggles behind the laments do not seem to be petty.* In today's society we are poised and ready to plunge into cynicism at the slightest disappointment in order that we may clench our teeth at someone and demand personal justice.

We cannot turn to the Old Testament's tragic poets to justify this self-righteous impulse to be offended and hurt.

The trials of those poets were not minor annoyances but grim crucibles that shoved the stench of death into their faces. The lament prayers are the longing groans of refugees of war. They are the frightful cries of those who felt illness sucking life from their bones and dragging them down to Sheol. Biblical laments are holocaust prayers, the prayers of those who can hear the rumbling machinery of war on the other side of the gate; they are the cries of those who hear armed men lusting for bloodshed on the other side of the door. The laments are the furious poetry of those whose hairs are bristling on the backs of their necks because they've seen the shredding of the poor with their own despairing eyes. They are the pleas of those who have been maliciously accused of murder and know they are innocent. They are the pleas of those who have murdered and know God has found them out. They are the spluttering moans of those who are wandering in a spiritual wasteland and can crawl no further through the dry gravel. These laments comprise the indignant questions of those who have seen the gaunt bodies of children writhing with hunger pangs from famine. These laments drip with the panicked tears of those who hear the growling of wild beasts snipping at their heels.

The tragic poets' prayers arise from trials that lie at the limits (and at times beyond the limits) of the bearable. Since these laments are canonized as Scripture, we can utilize them to give voice to our own sufferings; *yet we do so only with great care and respect.* The sacred language of biblical laments that have emerged from pestilence, from severe illness and from heart-stopping regret are not available for cynics who are just looking for any old ax to grind with God.

It must be repeated, however, that some of the more cynical among us have been so drastically banged up that they will find no greater source of catharsis than joining in the funereal choruses of those aching songs. And those who are singing triumphant melodies rather than dreary dirges, who are dancing and not mourning, must honor the space Scripture allots for squirming and agonizing before God. If we intend to drain the poison of cynicism from the church's veins, then we must learn to live with the grating wails of the sick and the sore and avoid forcing them to sing in a more melodious key. These disillusioned brothers and sisters may have no choir they can sing with other than the tragic poets, whose discordant voices we've muffled in our worship for so long.

DISCUSSION QUESTIONS

1. Describe a time when you attended a worship service that allowed for a time of lament.

2. Has there been a season or experience in your own life when the laments of Scripture ministered to you? If so, describe it.

3. Describe your response to the audacity of the lament prayers that appeared in this chapter.

4. How might being a Christian determine how we read the imprecatory prayers in the Old Testament?

5. Have you ever been angry with God? If so, how did you deal with that anger?

6. Why do you think it's so important to express our frustration, anger and disillusionment in the context of worship?

the way of
the christ

Sacrificial Embrace Instead of Cynical Rejection

Why did you spend so much?
Why did you give it all?
Poured out on cold little misers
And the returns are so small
Yeah those strange economics
And the length that love goes
Oh my blister soul

—Bill Mallonee, "Blister Soul (Reprise)"

What does it mean to recall the God who was crucified in a society
whose official creed is optimism, and which is knee-deep in blood. . . .
Jesus Christ died crying out "My God, my God, why has thou forsaken
me?" All Christian theology and all Christian life is basically an answer
to the question which Jesus asked as he died.

—Jürgen Moltmann, *The Crucified God*

Consider him who endured from sinners such hostility against himself,
so that you may not grow weary or fainthearted.

—Hebrews 12:3

We are faced with this wonderful, or not-so-wonderful irony: Jesus—
most admired, most worshiped (kind of), most written about. And least
followed.

—Eugene Peterson, *The Jesus Way*

Idol-casting is an obsolete trade now in the Western world, at least as a *manual* craft. Emotionally and theologically speaking, however, the guild of god-making is quite active. And as the trend usually goes, the mold we use for casting the object of our worship looks a lot like us ("You thought that I was just like you" [Psalm 50:21 NASB]).

Some years ago my wife was attending a Bible study when someone asked how Jesus' teaching could have been heard by such large crowds when there were no microphones or electronic amplification systems in first-century Palestine. Before anyone responded, he suggested his own tentative answer: "I think something supernatural was taking place because I just can't imagine Jesus being loud."

An alternative answer was then boisterously supplied from the other side of the room: "I don't think there was anything supernatural about that at all! I think of Jesus as having a real big mouth. He just spoke so loud everyone could hear him."

My wife noticed that the person who could not imagine Jesus being loud was a quiet introvert. The person who assumed Jesus had a big mouth was a talkative extrovert. Their instant interpretations of Jesus' public speaking ministry illustrates how easy we recast Jesus into our image.[1] The introvert wanted to worship a soft-spoken Jesus; the extrovert wanted a loud-mouthed Jesus. Much of our theology is a self-styled adaptation of God—our worship may at times amount to no more than the admiration of our own glamorized image in the mirror. Many Republicans assume Jesus would have voted for John McCain in the 2008 U.S. presidential election, and many Democrats assume he breathed a sigh of relief when Obama won. Mild-mannered folks who mind their own business envision Jesus as a calm, gentle teacher who would never have raised his voice or uttered threats. Malcontents view Jesus as a harsh anarchist whose inflammatory teaching was growled through clenched teeth or exclaimed with a clenched fist.

Of all the fanciful ideas about Jesus out there, "few are as misleading and distorted as the idea that Jesus was a Mediterranean Cynic."[2] Cynicism has been around for a long time, and in Jesus' day there were mendicant teachers schooled in its Greco-Roman version. The idea that Jesus should be numbered among these ancient world Cynics is most championed by a group of scholars known as the Jesus Seminar.[3] They are self-avowed skeptics. It is likely that their ideas amount to another case of recasting Jesus in the image of his onlookers.[4] Perhaps it takes a modern-day cynic to recognize an ancient one, but then again, even a cursory overview of the scholarship arrayed against the arguments renders the Jesus-was-a-Cynic idea outlandish.[5] He may have been sympathetic to some of the values of Greco-Roman Cynicism, but Jesus' teaching and lifestyle were not in keeping with the Cynics of his day. As we will see, he also cannot be categorized among the cynics of *our* day.

But even though Jesus was not a cynic in our sense of the term, he could have been one. It is hard to imagine a ministerial career quite so tragic and disillusioning.

WHY JESUS COULD HAVE EASILY BECOME CYNICAL

Why do I suggest that Jesus could have been a cynic? For starters, Jesus' reception could have been a bit more enthusiastic, especially considering the fact that the Messiah's arrival was so earnestly anticipated.

The bitter longings and passionate hopes of many first-century Jews were concentrated on the emergence of a new king out of the ashes of David's household: the Messiah (or Christ). Having endured centuries of political oppression since the exile, Jewish eyes were ever scanning the horizon for a royal hero. The years of waiting had so intensified the yearning that the appearance of the true, bona fide Messiah (there were a number of other contenders) should have been occasioned with historic fanfare. But "when the fullness of time had come" (Galatians 4:4), when the painstaking orchestration of God's divine plan had come at long last to the moment of sending the Christ, the reception was the opposite of what it should have been.

At his birth a handful of shepherds showed up, a couple of older folks got excited in the temple one day, and a strange entourage of Persian sages appeared later on bearing gifts; but the inns were full and, before long, armed men committed mass infanticide in Bethlehem's streets. The inhospitality that marked Jesus' birth continued throughout his public ministry. John's Gospel sums up Jesus' reception as the Messiah and Son of God: "The world was made through him, yet the world did not know him. He came to his own, and his own people did not receive him" (John 1:10-11).

Talk about a disillusioning career.

Sure, there was some initial enthusiasm after Jesus first got his ministry off the ground in Galilee. He was a fascinating teacher; he could tell a good story; and even more curious, he wielded special powers. Still, the crowds often sought him for misguided reasons: because they wanted revolutionary war (John 6:15), because he gave them food (John 6:25-27) or because he provided healing without pesky demands for quid pro quo service—some didn't even feel compelled to thank him (Luke 17:11-19). Those special powers, however, began generating a great deal of confusion and conflict—after healing the Gerasene demoniac, the locals "began to beg Jesus to depart from their region" (Mark 5:17), and once he was accused of casting out demons "by Beelzebul, the prince of demons" (Luke 11:15).

You would think things would fare better at home. Early in his Galilean ministry, Luke narrates how Jesus briefly suspended his travels for a quick visit with the folks back in Nazareth. The homecoming was so pleasant at first: "all spoke well of him and marveled at the gracious words that were coming from his mouth" (Luke 4:22), until he shared a few gracious words about Gentiles.

Then they tried to toss him off a cliff.

At least he had the disciples, right? Friends who would listen so attentively to all those gracious words and stick it out with him through thick and through thin:

> Do you not understand this parable? How then will you understand all the parables? (Mark 4:13)

> Do you not yet perceive or understand? Are your hearts hardened? (Mark 8:17)

When many of his disciples heard it, they said, "This is a hard saying; who can listen to it?" . . . After this many of his disciples turned back and no longer walked with him. (John 6:60, 66)

His family wasn't very supportive either. (Where were they when the neighbors were trying to drag him to the edge of that cliff?) John starkly reports that "not even his brothers believed in him" (John 7:5). At one point, his family actually "went out to seize him, for they were saying, 'He is out of his mind'" (Mark 3:21).

Even John the Baptist, Jesus' forerunner (and cousin)—the guy who baptized him and spoke so highly of him to the multitudes that had gathered alongside Jordan's banks—was unsure about Jesus: "Are you the one who is to come, or shall we look for another?" (Luke 7:20).

(Really, John?)

John may have been befuddled, but the religious leaders were downright incensed. Jesus' reception among the established elite was by far the least welcoming. Their gradual move from reluctant fascination to irritation and then to hateful contempt is carefully developed in all four Gospels. The Pharisees had appointed themselves as local guardians of the Jewish traditions, which Jesus came to clarify. The scribes and lawyers were meticulously reading the Scriptures, which Jesus came to fulfill. The uppity Sadducees were caretakers of the temple, which Jesus came to replace.

And they publicly harassed him and repeatedly sought his arrest.

At least he still had the disciples, those loyal companions whose grasp of his purpose and mission was so strong and encouraging.

Peter took him aside and began to rebuke him. But turning and seeing his disciples, he rebuked Peter and said, "Get behind me, Satan!" (Mark 8:32-33)

[The crowds] were bringing children to him that he might touch them, and the disciples rebuked them. But when Jesus saw it, he was indignant. (Mark 10:13-14)

Finally, when he came to Jerusalem (for the last time), he actually received red-carpet attention aptly fit for a king:

> And the crowds that went before him and that followed him
> were shouting, "Hosanna to the Son of David! Blessed is he who
> comes in the name of the Lord! Hosanna in the highest!" (Matthew 21:9)

This excitement (along with that stunt Jesus pulled in the temple),
however, served to exacerbate the religious leaders' resistance to him,
so they hatched a devious plan:

> Then the chief priests and the elders of the people gathered in
> the palace of the high priest, whose name was Caiaphas, and
> plotted together in order to arrest Jesus by stealth and kill him.
> (Matthew 26:3-4)

At least Jesus still had his disciples, those loyal followers who supported him with such inspiring devotion ("Then one of the twelve,
whose name was Judas Iscariot, went to the chief priests and said,
'What will you give me if I deliver him over to you?' " [Matthew 26:14-
15]). At least in the night of his fiercest torment Jesus could count on
his inner circle ("He came and found them sleeping. . . . [A]gain he
came and found them sleeping. . . . And he came the third time and
said to them, 'Are you still sleeping?' " [Mark 14:37, 40, 41]). At least
Peter, who had emphatically pledged to die with him (Mark 14:31),
would stand near at hand ("'I do not know this man of whom you
speak.' And immediately the rooster crowed" [Mark 14:71-72]).

And even though the reception earlier in the week had been so
positive by the crowds, when Pontius Pilate (with tongue in cheek)
proclaimed, "Behold your king!" the exuberant reply was not "Hosanna to the Son of David" but "We have no king but Caesar" (John
19:14, 15) and "Crucify, crucify him!" (Luke 23:21).

"We have no king but Caesar"—the crowd had the nerve to say
something like *that?* "Crucify, crucify him!"—*this* was their chant?
The disillusionment must have been breathtaking.

It was to get even worse, though. Much worse. Could there be a more disillusioning scene of mockery and spite than what occurred on Golgotha?

> Aha! You who would destroy the temple and rebuild it in three days, save yourself, and come down from the cross! (Mark 15:29-30)

> He saved others; he cannot save himself. Let the Christ, the King of Israel, come down now from the cross that we may see and believe. (Mark 15:31)

> If you are the King of the Jews, save yourself! (Luke 23:37)

> He trusts in God; let God deliver him now, if he desires him. For he said, "I am the Son of God." (Matthew 27:43)

In spite of all this derision, at least Jesus had God to rely on as an unswerving mainstay in the face of rejection. The people may have snubbed him as their Messiah, but at least Jesus could rest in the joyous reality that he was God's Son . . .

> My God, my God, why have you forsaken me? (Mark 15:34)

Concerning this appalling cry of dereliction, Jürgen Moltmann writes, "As a 'blasphemer,' Jesus was rejected by the guardians of his people's law. As a 'rebel,' he was crucified by the Romans. But finally, and most profoundly, he died as one rejected by his God and Father."[6]

If anyone in our Scriptures had a right to be cynical toward God's people, it is the One who suffered most unjustly at their hands and yet gave more than anyone else on their behalf. If anyone had a right to be cynical with God, it is the One who suffered the most excruciating divine abandonment ever and yet deserved it the least.

Can anyone justify being a cynic if Jesus was not a cynic?

JESUS AND THE WAYS OF WISDOM, PROPHETIC PROTEST AND LAMENT

This book has two purposes. The first is to contend that cynicism is the wrong way to respond to our disappointments and frustrations with God and the church. But since the disillusioning falsehoods and disenfranchising practices of the church *must* be subverted and confronted, the second purpose of the book is to present biblical ways to respond *constructively*. The foremost way commended to us is the way of Jesus, who was *not* an unthreatening, complacent keeper of the peace who refused to ruffle feathers; instead he was an alarming reformer who forcefully critiqued social and religious misdeeds and falsehoods. So we now turn to see how Jesus exemplified a ministry of subversion and confrontation, embodying the ways of the sages, prophets and tragic poets while also expanding and reshaping their approaches.

1. *Jesus and the way of the sage.* Mary and Joseph surely struggled with a tremendous degree of anxiety and insecurity over being entrusted with raising the Messiah. So they must have been beside themselves with misery when they once realized that little Jesus was not in the caravan making its way back to Nazareth from Jerusalem. (How would *you* feel if you lost God's Son?) The frantic searching came to an end in the temple, where they found the boy "sitting with the teachers, listening to them and asking them questions" (Luke 2:46). If you lose a twelve-year-old, the last place you might search would be a library or a classroom, but the only glimpse we have of Jesus' boyhood in the Gospels shows us that he was a voracious learner who identified himself with the teachers of Israel (who, by the way, were "amazed at his understanding and his answers" [Luke 2:47]). Luke brackets the account telling us that, as a child, Jesus was "filled with wisdom" (Luke 2:40) and that, as a maturing adolescent, he "increased in wisdom" (Luke 2:52). From childhood Jesus was well on his way to becoming a sage in the wisdom traditions of his religious heritage.

Disciples and bystanders alike addressed him as "Teacher," a title Jesus embraced for himself (Matthew 26:18). Flipping through the pages of any Bible that prints the words of Jesus in red will demonstrate just how significant teaching was in Jesus' ministry. Before the tables turned in Nazareth and the hometown folks took offense at him, they were "astonished" and asked, "Where did this man get these things? What is the wisdom given to him?" (Mark 6:2; cf. Matthew 13:54). In keeping with the Old Testament sages, Jesus' wisdom teaching was countercultural. During one of the feasts in Jerusalem the chief priests and Pharisees were so offended by his teaching they sent officers to arrest Jesus. When they came back empty-handed (and perhaps wide-eyed), the leaders demanded an explanation as to why they did not have Jesus in bonds; their bedazzled reply was "No one ever spoke like this man!" (John 7:46). Jesus taught as a brilliant and controversial sage.

Like the sages before him, Jesus employed riddles, aphorisms and parabolic stories to critique pop theology and assault empty religious performance.[7] He took popular notions of the law and then turned them on their heads ("you have heard that it was said . . . but I say to you . . ."—this appears throughout Matthew 5:21-43). He did not shrink back from decrying false trends and theological distortions, but he did so through creative teaching pregnant with divine wisdom. Just as Qoholeth and the author of Job wrote to upturn conventional wisdom, Jesus' words demanded "a paradigm shift of colossal proportions."[8]

The confrontational nature of his teaching is best seen in his interrogatory response to the religious leaders during the last week of his life. Just as God silenced Job's questions with questions of his own, Jesus silenced the scribes, priests and lawyers by responding to their questions with even better questions. This continued until finally "no one was able to answer him a word, nor from that day did anyone dare to ask him any more questions" (Matthew 22:46). His brilliant didactics clearly placed Jesus among the celebrated sages of Israel's past.

But Jesus was much more than just a sage:

> The queen of the South will rise up at the judgment with this generation and condemn it, for she came from the ends of the earth to hear the wisdom of Solomon, and behold, something greater than Solomon is here. (Matthew 12:42)

John tells us that Jesus was the "Word" and that the "Word became flesh" (John 1:1-14). Wisdom could be personified in ancient writings and associated with the concept of "Word" (*logos* in the Greek). Jesus was not only a sage, but One "greater than Solomon," who came as the very embodiment of divine Wisdom.

As we wrestle today with the church's misconceptions and faulty theologies, we learn from Jesus the inestimable worth of sound, wise teaching grounded in Scripture. Jesus was unafraid to challenge his hearers with his knowledge, but he also knew when to hold back—"I have many things to say to you, but you cannot bear them now" (John 16:12). He did not exploit the masses with his superior intelligence. He did not delight in academic pedigrees, nor would he be impressed with the fancy academic titles we use today:

> The Jews therefore marveled, saying, "How is it that this man has learning, when he has never studied?" So Jesus answered them, "My teaching is not mine, but his who sent me." (John 7:15-16)

> But you are not to be called rabbi, for you have one teacher, and you are all brothers. And call no man your father on earth, for you have one Father, who is in heaven. Neither be called instructors, for you have one instructor, the Christ. The greatest among you shall be your servant. Whoever exalts himself will be humbled, and whoever humbles himself will be exalted. (Matthew 23:8-12)

The scene from Jesus' boyhood encourages us to be exceptional students of wisdom and intimately conversant with the Scriptures. Mary and Joseph saw that Jesus yearned to remain "in my Father's house" (Luke 2:49), surrounded by all that exhilarating teaching, but he did not embrace a pedantic life confined to ivory towers. He took his wisdom to fishing shores and dusty streets. As the preeminent Sage, his example challenges us to avoid intellectual banter behind closed doors (or behind the backs of the untrained) and to actively engage the people of God with strong, focused teaching that undermines falsehood and promotes truth.

2. Jesus and the way of the prophet. Jesus identified himself as a prophet as well as a teacher (Mark 6:4). This seems to be how he was most widely viewed by the public: " 'Who do people say that the Son of Man is?' And they said, 'Some say John the Baptist, others say Elijah, and others Jeremiah or one of the prophets" (Matthew 16:13-14; cf. Matthew 21:11, 26).

We saw in chapter eleven that prophets were marginalized figures. In keeping with this tendency, we find in Matthew that from the moment of his birth Jesus was being shoved to the fringes by the political establishment. After rushing off to Egypt, Joseph had to eventually settle his little family in the backwater margins of Galilee because of jealousy in the courts of Jerusalem, that fateful "city that kills the prophets" (Luke 13:34). Years later, Jesus was sent before Herod Antipas (a son of Herod the Great, the king who had sponsored the Bethlehem child murders). This new king had already dispensed with John the Baptist and his inconvenient protests, and he seemed to have no trouble with Pilate, the face of imperial governance in Palestine, signing Jesus' execution orders. Jesus knew well the politically enforced fringe existence of a prophet.

He also manifested a rough-edged prophetic disposition. Many of us have adopted a "Mr. Nice Guy" persona for Jesus. We love that gentle scene alluded to earlier where he is holding and blessing babies. But even in that sweet moment Jesus is "indignant" when he sees his disciples chasing off the little kids (Mark 10:14). Babies in his arms or not, Jesus could be frictional and abrasive.

Thrown into the mix of his subversive teaching about the leadership establishment were direct verbal assaults in keeping with the prophetic tradition. This may be disturbing to our modern sensibilities, but Jesus actually called people names. He called the religious leaders a "brood of vipers" (Matthew 12:34; 23:33; cf. Matthew 3:7; Luke 3:7); "hypocrites" (several times in Matthew 23 alone); and "fools" (Matthew 23:17; cf. Luke 11:40). When someone once brought up Herod Antipas, Jesus said, "Go and tell that fox . . ." (Luke 13:32).

This name-calling was not just rhetorical—Jesus was genuinely angry and exasperated at times:

190 FAITH WITHOUT ILLUSIONS

And he looked around at them with anger, grieved at their hard-
ness of heart. (Mark 3:5)

The Pharisees came and began to argue with him, seeking
from him a sign from heaven to test him. And he sighed deeply
in his spirit and said, "Why does this generation seek a sign?
Truly, I say to you, no sign will be given to this generation."
(Mark 8:11-12)

He had the audacity to look the Sadducees in the face and tell them
"You are wrong, because you know neither the Scriptures nor the
power of God" (Matthew 22:29), and he actually told a group of Jewish leaders, "You are of your father the devil" (John 8:44). The prophetic vehemence of Jesus may be most evident in the many "woes"
he pronounced in harsh judgment of those religious leaders (and of a
few unreceptive cities: Chorazin, Bethsaida and Capernaum [Luke
10:13-15]). Matthew 23 contains the most detailed account of Jesus'
woes to the "scribes and Pharisees" (see also Luke 11:37-54). Seven
times he blasted these religious figureheads with invective, even as-
signing them the bloodguilt of all the murdered prophets in Israel's
checkered religious history.

His impassioned frustrations went beyond words into actions. Old
Testament prophets were known to perform symbolic acts that dra-
matized their oracles of impending judgment. Jesus was operating out
of this tradition when he cursed a fig tree (Mark 11:12-25) and then
stormed the temple and commenced to tossing tables, flinging coins
and shouting at merchants. John tells us that Jesus even wielded a
"whip of cords" during the boisterous ruckus (John 2:15).

Does this sound like the Christ we gather to worship on Sunday
mornings?

A cynical reader of the Gospels may readily identify with these
disturbing scenes of Jesus as a prophetic agitator. We are not to dismiss the edginess of our Lord. His heated confrontations ever remind
us that we are not to turn a blind eye to theological distortions, ethical
failures or rampant religiosity.

But Jesus was more *anguished* than *angry* throughout his ministry. In studying "the way of the prophet," we saw in chapter eight that compassion and sympathy undergirded the frustration and fury of God's prophets. The same was true in the ministry of Jesus.

The seven judgments of Matthew 23 are followed by a prophetic lament so poignant with grief that we must read the woe pronouncements as coming from the lips of a broken, mourning shepherd:

O Jerusalem, Jerusalem, you who kill the prophets and stone those sent to you, how often I have longed to gather your children together, as a hen gathers her chicks under her wings, but you were not willing. (Matthew 23:37 NIV; cf. Luke 13:34-35)

By ending the woes with imagery of maternal longing, it is clear that "the woes were uttered in regret, that the indignation was righteous."[9] The picture of a mother hen stretching out her wings to draw her helpless little ones into the safety of her breast betokens a Savior whose arms are aching from being outstretched for so long. His disappointment in his people is only as acute as his *love* for his people.

Just before Jesus delivered his woe pronouncements, Luke tells us that his final pilgrimage to Jerusalem was marked by painful grief:

And when he drew near and saw the city, he wept over it, saying, "Would that you, even you, had known on this day the things that make for peace! But now they are hidden from your eyes. For the days will come upon you, when your enemies will set up a barricade around you and surround you and hem you in on every side and tear you down to the ground, you and your children within you. And they will not leave one stone upon another in you, because you did not know the time of your visitation." (Luke 19:41-44)

About forty years later, the Roman military juggernaut would grind Jerusalem and the temple into dust and ash. Unlike Jonah, perched outside of Nineveh and hoping for destruction, Jesus was longingly eyeing Jerusalem and bemoaning that the destruction was inevitable.

Before cynics exalt Jesus as their hero for so smartly bashing the religious folks, they need to strain their ears to hear him weeping on the outskirts of doomed Jerusalem.

It is true that Jesus was, at times, disappointed with the masses (Mark 9:19; Luke 11:29), but primarily we see him moved with pity and compassion for them:

When he saw the crowds, he had compassion for them, because they were harassed and helpless, like sheep without a shepherd. (Matthew 9:36)

When he went ashore he saw a great crowd, and he had compassion on them, because they were like sheep without a shepherd. And he began to teach them many things. (Mark 6:34)

I have compassion on the crowd, because they have been with me now three days and have nothing to eat. And if I send them away hungry to their homes, they will faint on the way. And some of them have come from far away. (Mark 8:2)

Before cynics cross their arms in glowering disapproval and begin distancing themselves from the church, they need to notice the way Jesus looked at the bedraggled and misguided masses, and how he could hardly repress the impulse to serve them even when he was exhausted. As the prophets before him, Jesus was emotionally invested in the welfare of God's people in spite of their failures and misunderstandings.

But Jesus was much more than just a prophet:

The men of Nineveh will rise up at the judgment with this generation and condemn it, for they repented at the preaching of Jonah, and behold, something greater than Jonah is here. (Matthew 12:41)

Then turning to the disciples he said privately, "Blessed are the eyes that see what you see! For I tell you that many prophets and kings desired to see what you see, and did not see it, and to hear what you hear, and did not hear it." (Luke 10:23-24)

Jesus refused to distance himself from the messy issues of his people. He entered into their pain and misery, taking on their flesh, paying the taxes they had to pay and, beyond the work of any prophet before him, he ultimately took within himself even their sin.

3. *Jesus and the way of the tragic poet.* The suffering that attended Jesus' taking into himself the sins of his people is where we most clearly see him identifying with the cries of lament haunting the Psalms, Job, Lamentations and the Prophets. But before those final twenty-four hours when the despair of being "the Lamb of God, who takes away the sin of the world" (John 1:29) became so unbearable, we find Jesus answering appeals and pleas that could have come straight out of the lament poems:

> And a leper came to him, imploring him, and kneeling said to him, "If you will, you can make me clean." (Mark 1:40)

> Teacher, do you not care that we are perishing? (Mark 4:38)

> Jairus . . . fell at his feet and implored him earnestly, saying, "My little daughter is at the point of death. Come and lay your hands on her, so that she may be made well and live." (Mark 5:22-23)

> If you can do anything, have compassion on us and help us. (Mark 9:22)

> Have mercy on me! (Mark 10:47)

> Lord, save me. (Matthew 14:30)

Jesus' compassionate response to those who cried out in distress is consistent with the openness of Yahweh to receive the cries of Israel in the Old Testament laments.[10]

Jesus was not just answering appeals, though. He was also found making them.

The disciples must have detected their Lord's foreboding sense of apprehension as they reclined at the table for their final meal together. The tension was broken (yet then intensified), I suppose, when he said, "One of you will betray me, one who is eating with me" (Mark 14:18). After supper he had to break more disconcerting news to them: "You will all fall away" (Mark 14:27); and to Peter: "You will deny me three times" (Mark 14:30). Jesus could intimately relate to those tragic poets who wrote about the betrayal of their closest allies and friends.

Later on in Gethsemane's darkness we see how Jesus could also relate to the awful experience of God's distance. "Greatly distressed and troubled," he confided to Peter, James and John that his soul was "very sorrowful, even to death" (Mark 14:33-34). And then, while those closest friends drifted off to sleep, Jesus made his appeal to heaven, sweating droplets of blood, "being in an agony" (Luke 22:44).

I do not know how to write about that night in Gethsemane. I do not know what to say about the agony of the Christ, whose fervent, gut-wrenching prayers were so bluntly rejected. Nor do I know how to write about what happened to Jesus the next day—the nails, the wooden beams, the scowling faces, the sour wine, the pleated thorn crown, the nakedness, the open wounds, the scourge of noontime darkness. I do not know what to say about what took place between Jesus and his Father through the portentous sky, that "God against God" moment that ended with a "loud cry" (Mark 15:37).[11]

It was no triumphant victory shout. In Mark's account Jesus cried out with a "loud voice/cry" twice while on the cross (Mark 15:34, 37). These shouts echo the two other instances where we read "loud voice" earlier in the Gospel—they are the screeching protests of rejected demons (Mark 1:26; 5:7).[12] According to Mark, when Jesus died, it was with a raucous death howl.

I do not know how to write about that awful sound and that terrible sight. The sight and sound on which Christians have founded their faith. But when we have no words yet must somehow say something in such darkness, we may turn to the laments just as Jesus did, when in his first awful shout he "cried with a loud voice, . . . 'My God, my God, why have you forsaken me?' " (Mark 15:34; cf. Psalm 22:1). To give voice to the horror of the moment, Jesus embraced the tragic poetry of Israel's hymn book.

But Jesus was more than a tragic poet.

He ventured beyond the misery of normal human existence into unchartered torment. He ventured into the torment of unjustified abandonment by the Father with whom he was one (John 10:30); he ventured into the torment of the God-beloved becoming the God-forsaken. The tragic poets knew what it felt like to be abandoned by God. But none of them knew the nightmare of being *God* abandoned by *God*.

Psalm 22 eventually transitions into hopeful praise. Did Jesus make that transition on the cross? It is hard to say from Mark's account. The experiential transition from despair to praise would have to wait three more days. Three days after the bystanders heard him eerily cry out in agony with his final breath. It sounded like a terrified demon in flight.

SACRIFICIAL EMBRACE INSTEAD OF CYNICAL REJECTION

Though in Mark we find Jesus dying with a lament psalm fresh on his famished lips, there is a striking distinction between Jesus and the Old Testament tragic poets: *He did not pray imprecatory prayers.*[13] Never had anyone been more justified in praying for vengeance and vindication than Jesus while he hung before the Golgotha mockers— but no appeal for retribution was made from the cross.

Now, there are some echoes from psalms with imprecations earlier in Mark's account of Jesus' final twenty-four hours (i.e., Psalm 41; 69).[14] And Jesus was certainly strident in his confrontations that week, crying out woes, throwing merchants out of the temple and cursing fruitless trees. Yet he never directly prayed that God would attack his enemies. Not even during the shame and hurt of his arrest, trial and crucifixion. There were plenty of laments from the Psalter that Jesus could have cried out.

He chose Psalm 22. There are no imprecations in Psalm 22.

Jesus was introducing a new ethic, the way of his emerging kingdom, *the way of the Christ*.

Though they had been taught "an eye for an eye," Jesus told them instead to turn the other cheek to the one who slaps their face (Matthew 5:38-39). Though they had been taught to "hate your enemy," Jesus told them instead to *love* their enemies and to *pray* for them (Matthew 5:43-44; cf. Luke 6:27-36). When the sons of Zebedee wanted to call down the fire of God from heaven on a Samaritan village that rejected them (no room in many inns for Jesus), they were rebuked (Luke 9:54-55). When a disciple sliced an ear off a member of the arresting posse in Gethsemane, Jesus said "No more of this!" and healed the man's gaping wound (Luke 22:50-51).

During Lent one year, I was reading the crucifixion scene to my son. At age four he had already learned from preschool what it is like to be picked on and chided by others. I asked him, "If you were as powerful and mighty as Jesus, what would you do if those bad-guy soldiers put you on a cross while those mean priests made fun of you?"

"I know what I would do," he replied in his tiny, earnest voice. "I would come down off that cross and get those mean guys and beat them up!"

So would I, little fellow. If I am honest, so would I.

The most compelling action from the life of Jesus for cynics to ponder is not his cleansing of the temple or his cursing of the fruitless fig tree—it is his *inaction* on the cross. Behold the restraint of Jesus when they mocked his captivity to a cross he could have splintered and consumed in heavenly fire, yet he did not. He could have prayed for legions of angels to appear with flaming swords (Matthew 26:53), yet he did not. And instead of praying an imprecatory prayer, Luke writes that he prayed, "Father, forgive them, for they know not what they do" (Luke 23:34).

If there is anyone who deserved to be cynical, it was the guy with Gentile spittle running down his beard and his nation's demands for his death ringing in his ears. But Jesus was not a cynic. If he had been a cynic, Jesus would not have given his life for crowds that said things like "We have no king but Caesar." If he had been a cynic, Jesus would not have given his life for friends he saw scatter in disloyal cowardice the night before. A cynic would not die for misguided masses gorging themselves with pop theology. A cynic would not die for pompous religious leaders drunk with power and blinded to their religiosity. A cynic would have crossed his arms and turned away in hurtful anger. But Jesus arms were fixed to a cross and splayed wide open.

What if Jesus had allowed the physical pain of the punches, the lashes and the asphyxiating tug of his weight on the spikes to have crushed his intentions to love a people who had inflicted him with the emotional pain of abandonment, rejection and denial? What if he had permitted his brokenness to have soured into such a begrudging bitterness that instead of enduring death as the sacrificial Lamb of God, he ripped himself off the cross as a warlike Lion of Judah? What if Jesus had become cynical and changed his mind about embracing us in love?

> For one will scarcely die for a righteous person—though perhaps for a good person one would dare even to die—but God shows his love for us in that while we were still sinners, Christ died for us. (Romans 5:7-8)

Instead of cynical rejection, Jesus offered sacrificial embrace.

And he did not just die for misguided masses and self-righteous legalists. Jesus did not just die for reality-denying idealists. He did not just die for sensationalists who are always demanding signs and wonders. He did not just die for traditionalists who can't relate to their (Hellenized or secularized) culture. He did not just die for anti-intellectuals who resist paradigm shifts. He also died for cynics.

Only a noncynic would die for a cynic.

It would seem that, for Jesus, the best way to deal with adherents to pop theology, legalists, idealists and cynics alike is to suffer and die on their behalf. This is the way of the Christ.

DISCUSSION QUESTIONS

1. Like those in the Bible study mentioned at the beginning of the chapter, name a trait that you envision you and Jesus sharing. How accurate is your assumption?

2. At what point in Jesus' life do you think it was most difficult for
   him to resist the temptation to become cynical? How do you think
   you would have responded?

3. Which of the three "ways" Jesus lived most challenges you: Jesus
   as Sage (full of wisdom), Jesus as Prophet (addressing sin and error) or Jesus as Poet (entering the pain of the laments)?

4. When you consider those you are most cynical toward, are you
   willing to offer the type of sacrificial embrace that Christ displayed?
   Why or why not?

5. How does Jesus' crucifixion affect the way you respond to those
   who have hurt you and left you disillusioned?

12

on the roads
to emmaus
and damascus

Resurrection, Paul and Hopeful Realism

When I saw him, I fell at his feet as
though dead. But he laid his right
hand on me, saying, "Fear not, I am the
first and the last, and the living one. I died,
and behold I am alive forevermore, and I have the
keys of Death and Hades."

Revelation 1:17-18

Finally, brothers, whatever is true, whatever is honorable, whatever is
just, whatever is pure, whatever is lovely, whatever is commendable, if
there is any excellence, if there is anything worthy of praise, think
about these things.

Philippians 4:8

God will redeem the whole universe; Jesus's resurrection is the
beginning of that new life, the fresh grass growing through the
concrete of corruption and decay in the old world.

—N. T. Wright, *Surprised by Hope*

We do not know why they are heading for Emmaus. We just know *how* they are heading there. Demoralized and deflated, the two disciples are trudging along a rocky road leading away from Jerusalem.

Away from Jerusalem.

Away from the noise of mobs demanding blood. Away from the sight of cruciform posts with dangling bodies.

"What are you two talking about?"

An interruption. The question freezes their pace. The traveler had been edging closer to them as they walked. They are in no mood for an eavesdropper, but one of the disciples, Cleopas, decides to speak. It is not a very chatty response: "Are you the only visitor to Jerusalem who does not know what has happened?"

"Fill me in."

They tell the man about Jesus of Nazareth. He had been an impressive fellow, doing and saying stuff like no one else. Died not more than three days ago. "We had hoped that he was the one to redeem Israel."

We had hoped.

"I might add something," the disciple volunteered, "something odd. Some women we know were making wild claims just before we left town, claims about seeing angels and not being able to find his body. Not sure what that's all about."

Missing corpse? Yeah, whatever.

We had hoped.

RESURRECTION AND THE END OF CYNICISM

The most classic expression of disillusionment in the Bible may well be those words of Cleopas on the Emmaus Road: "We had hoped that he was the one to redeem Israel" (Luke 24:21). He and the other disciples had been cheated. Cheated in the grandest way possible. Anxious longings for salvation that had intensified through the centuries, longings that had been beating wildly in the disciples' hearts—all that dreaming and hoping had come to the bursting point when, suddenly, a convincing candidate appeared. A possible savior. A potential king. One in whom all the remaining tatters of burning hopefulness might actually be realized. And then, outside the gates of the great city, the center of the world, the seat of David's throne and the locus of Yahweh's Shekinah presence, outside those gates the hoping against all hope came to a mocking, brutal end, with the clank of a hammer and a spike.

This is the kind of disillusionment that warrants—even demands—cynicism. When the limp, cold corpse of the architect of the most monumental salvation project in history is placed in the dark of a tomb, cynicism becomes more than just a right. It becomes a duty.

We had hoped.

But wait. An interruption. A stranger along the road. An unexpected interlocutor.

"What are you two talking about?"

We had hoped.

O foolish ones, and slow of heart to believe! (Luke 24:25)

When a dead man climbs out of his grave, something is happening. Something new. When a dead man opens his mouth to speak, something is underway. Something decisive. When a dead man chimes in and interrupts your cynical conversation, nothing can be the same again, ever.

There is no disillusionment too abject for the power and wonder of resurrection. There is no monstrous roaring too loud for the rising voice of the risen Christ. To the powers of hell, death, Leviathan and chaos that have repeatedly smashed our hopes and left us gutted and disillusioned in the dust—to these powers Easter proclaims, "Not much longer."

Resurrection announces the end of cynicism. And the end of cynicism will sound like this:

O death, where is your victory?
O death, where is your sting?
(1 Corinthians 15:55; cf. Isaiah 25:8; Hosea 13:14)

Resurrection announces the end of cynicism because it heralds the end of all that makes us cynical. The old age of sin and death, thorns and thistles, disorder and disillusionment—it entered its dusk on the dawn of the third day. Satan is weeping and gnashing his teeth. Death is choking on its own death rattle. And the sweet fragrance of new creation is rising from the blank emptiness of Jesus' grave. Resurrection renders cynicism obsolete. Cynicism is no longer necessary in the face of death's impending death and with the light of new creation shining out in the distance and in our midst.

In the opening chapter of this book, we observed that Eden brackets our Bibles. Idealists pretend they have one foot just inside Eden's door, but the cynics know better. The cynics know that the door back to the Garden is slammed shut. Rumor has it that an angel—not one to trifle with—stands guard. No return flights are available. What cynics *do not* seem to acknowledge, however, is that the remaking of Eden is on the horizon and in process. The river, the tree, the face of God. It will all be there—renewed and re-presented intact and without blemish. "And he who was seated on the throne said, 'Behold, I am making all things new'" (Revelation 21:5). The resurrection of Jesus signifies that new creation is around the corner. It also signifies that new creation has already begun. Already but not yet.

I am contending for "hopeful realism." This is a perspective that embraces the dual realities of contemporary evil and forthcoming redemption. It lives in the tension of creation's groaning and its imminent restoration. Idealists claim that we are in the suburbs of Eden. Cynics claim that Eden is a farce. Hopeful realists claim with joy that a new Eden is just around the corner and that fresh green sprouts are faintly pushing up through the cracks and crevices even now. Hopeful realists are still groaning with all of creation, but they can detect in the air that sweet fragrance of renewal released by the opening of Christ's tomb. The Fall in Genesis 3 nullifies idealism. New creation nullifies cynicism.

Christ's resurrection is the signature of new creation. It claims that nothing is irredeemable. *Nothing.* Cynics may protest that a perspective of already but not yet is simply not good enough for life lived in the present. But the drama narrated throughout Scripture pressures us to live in the present in light of the future. To make matters even better, the New Testament clarifies that tomorrow is ever encroaching backward into today. When we believe that new creation is in the works and on the way, then a daring hopefulness infuses our experience of daily reality, even when that reality is steeped in the broken mess of the old age, kicking and screaming in its waning hour.

THE OVERLAP OF AGES: HOW RESURRECTION RESETS OUR CLOCKS

I have become convinced that our understanding of the New Testament is severely limited without an awareness of the eschatological framework that makes hopeful realism both possible and necessary. The idea of an "overlap of the ages" was first broached in chapter three, but it is time for a closer look.

In Genesis 3, eschatological hope—a hope for God to bring about some work of redemption in the future—became an incipient necessity. After Adam and Eve took from the tree and ate, sin ripped a gash into the fabric of God's resplendent creation, through which death and sin made their unwelcome entry. To our great relief Scripture's overarching story gradually reveals the shockingly good news that God is not only the Creator but also the *Re*-creator. The One who made all things "good" will one day make all things "new." During the latter days of the monarchies in Israel and Judah, eschatology became increasingly important—the evidence was beginning to convey that a divine interruption of exceptional scope was required for rescuing humanity from its plight.[1] The exile in Babylon, along with the less-than-glorious restoration of Jerusalem and the temple, eventually generated apocalypticism, a heightened eschatological perspective that revealed heavenly realities behind the scenes of an unbearable status quo.

Surely, there awaits a day—*the Day.*

By the time Jesus was rising from the baptismal waters of the Jordan, faithful Jews were anticipating a cataclysmic Day of the Lord that would end the "present evil age" (Galatians 1:4) and inaugurate the "age to come" (Mark 10:30). This new age was associated with a range of variables that could include peace (shalom), salvation, the outpouring of the Spirit, the reign of the Messiah, divine judgment, the repentance of Gentiles and Isaiah's vision of new creation (Isaiah 65:17; 66:22).[2]

By the time of Jesus' ministry, a critical element that had become associated with new creation was *the resurrection of the dead*—God would not only re-create heaven and earth, but also the faithful who had been swallowed by death.[3] Jesus' emergence from the grave was therefore a surprising instance of the future age lurching backward into the present setting. Paul writes that "Christ has been raised from the dead, the firstfruits of those who have fallen asleep" (1 Corinthians 15:20). *Firstfruits* refers to the initial batch of the harvest, which signals that the rest of the harvest is soon on its way. Christ's resurrection has jumpstarted new creation in our current sphere, requiring an adjustment of the eschatological framework represented by figure 12.1 to that represented by figure 12.2.[4]

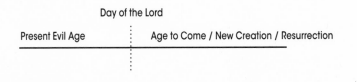

Figure 12.1. The old view

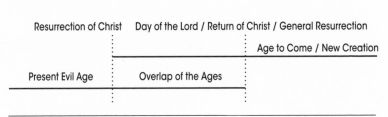

Figure 12.2. The already-but-not-yet view

Remember that odd scene in John's Gospel when the resurrected Christ breathes on his disciples and tells them to receive the Holy Spirit (John 20:22)? This is a reenactment of Genesis 2:7 when God breathed his "breath of life" (the word for "breath" here in the Hebrew can also mean "Spirit") into dust and created Adam. Jesus is God's agent of new creation. The consummation awaits his return (the parousia), so for the time being we live in this awkward overlap of the ages. Chaos and Satan still screech and howl, but amid the din of death there is a new sound, the new age's sweet melody, the faint but lovely tune that preludes joyful trumpet blasts.

Those who lack ears to hear this melody will be cynics. Those who hum along while groaning with creation are hopeful realists.

The eschatological framework I have sketched demands what Michael Gorman calls a life of " 'bifocality': living in the overlap of the ages by looking back to Christ's cross and resurrection and ahead to the parousia, general resurrection, judgment, and eternal life."[5] Such a bifocal perspective enables us to endure grim, disillusioning trials with joyous hope.

What does the bifocality of hopeful realism look like when practiced within everyday church life? We have studied patterns of instruction in the prophets, sages, psalmists and Jesus, none of whose ministries occurred within the context of ecclesial life. For a brief glimpse of a hopeful realist who worked specifically with localized Christian communities, let's turn to Saul of Tarsus, who like the two disciples in Luke 24, found himself face to face with the resurrected Christ on an ancient highway.

PRACTICING HOPEFUL REALISM WITH PAUL

We know why he is heading for Damascus. And we know *how* he is heading for Damascus. Indignant and enraged ("still breathing threats and murder" [Acts 9:1]), he trudges along a rocky road leading away from Jerusalem.

Away from Jerusalem.

Away from the noise of heretics preaching Jesus. Away from the sight of uneducated men pointing fingers at the high priest.

"Why are you persecuting me?"

An interruption. The question freezes his pace. The voice and the blinding light erupt out of nowhere.

Emmaus bound, Cleopas and his companion were found downcast and depressed. Damascus bound, Saul was zealous and confident. The encounter with Jesus left the disciples overjoyed. It left Saul blind enough to see his spiritual blindness. How disillusioning to discover that your religious vocation is entirely devoted to destroying the God you think you serve.

Whatever disillusionment he may have experienced, Saul of Tarsus emerged from the dust to eventually become the person we know as Paul the apostle. Though the biblical drama comprises only flawed characters in its cast (excluding One), Paul has no problem presenting himself as a role model. This is because he painfully and completely devoted his life to following the way of Jesus: "Be imitators of me, as I am of Christ" (1 Corinthians 11:1; cf. 1 Corinthians 4:16-17; 1 Thessalonians 1:6). Let's take Paul's command to heart in order to see how we might practically live as hopeful realists.

1. Struggling with churches: The indicative and the imperative. We tend to idealize the early church when we study the book of Acts. Reading the Pauline epistles reveals another side of the coin. The early Christians performed miracles and proclaimed the gospel with supernatural boldness and prayed until the walls shook. They also struggled with divorce, sexual immorality, cultural assimilation, religiosity, traditionalism, racism and social elitism as much as Christians today. The stinking pastoral messes that Paul faced could have easily incited him to check out of ministry as a jaded cynic. Betrayed, beaten, sleepless and unthanked, it is a wonder that he never seemed to experience apostolic burnout. Instead, we find him tirelessly devoted to lovingly (yet firmly) correcting the churches and individuals under his care.

The church in Galatia was one that had the potential to send him plummeting downward into cynical despair. Midway through the epistle he sent their way is the exasperated outcry, "O foolish Galatians! Who has bewitched you?" (Galatians 3:1). After all his pains-taking teaching, they had exchanged the gospel for blasphemous distortions. He rhetorically wonders if perhaps he "labored over [them] in vain" (Galatians 4:11). His frustration is so intense that he infamously expresses the wish that "those who unsettle you would emasculate themselves!" (Galatians 5:12).

Clearly, Paul's ministry does not suggest that we neglect engaging God's people when they are misguided. But even in his most furious moments Paul envisions himself not as an assailant "breathing threats and murder against the disciples of the Lord" (Acts 9:1). He had abandoned that vocational disposition on the road between Jerusalem and Damascus. Instead, he envisions himself as a parent loyally invested in the well-being of those under his pastoral wings, as if they were "my little children, for whom I am again in the anguish of childbirth until Christ is formed in you!" (Galatians 4:19; cf. 1 Thessalonians 2:5-8; Philippians 1:8). Paul rigorously corrected wayward churches, but not as a distanced, indifferent cynic who lobbed criticisms from the fringes.

The church in Corinth provided another severe test of Paul's patience. He had labored extensively among them for months. At some point after his ministry took him elsewhere, he began receiving reports of internal divisions, rank immorality, hyper-spirituality, twisted theology. He addressed these concerns in 1 Corinthians, but his ministry soon came under attack by "super-apostles" who exalted themselves as superior to Paul and stole away a number of the Corinthians' hearts (see 2 Corinthians 11). Second Corinthians provides a case study for seeking reconciliation with a church that has spurned us.

Between 1 Corinthians and 2 Corinthians Paul had sent another letter, which has not survived. It was apparently brutal. But he did not write to spitefully attack them: "I wrote to you out of much affliction and anguish of heart and with many tears, not to cause you pain but to let you know the abundant love that I have for you" (2 Corinthians 2:4).

Is this the normal attitude we take when confronting churches today? Do we admonish more out of disgust or out of a love so strong that we can say with Paul, "I will most gladly spend and be spent for your souls"? (2 Corinthians 12:15). Even among the dysfunctional Corinthians, Paul exemplifies a ministry that is constructive and not destructive, one that is "for building up and not for tearing down" (2 Corinthians 13:10).

How did he evade cynicism in the midst of these (and many more) hurtful struggles?

In spite of the disillusioning experiences with his local churches, Paul could cast a vision for a magnificent new humanity being renewed "in Christ" while all hell was breaking loose around them and within them. He preached that they were "new creations" (2 Corinthians 5:17; Galatians 6:15; cf. Colossians 3:9-10), yet at the same time he had to address ethical failings of outrageous proportions. He was able to embrace the tension of such sharp contrasts because he was a hopeful realist. Grasped by the eschatological framework reordered by Jesus' resurrection, he knew that the eternal life of new creation had to be lived in the overlap of the ages. Living as new creations in this awkward time frame does not mean the "groaning" (Romans 8:18-24) is silenced. But it does mean that our groaning points to something, to a "newness of life" (Romans 6:4) that can be experienced now through the Spirit.

Scholars refer to the *indicative* and the *imperative* dimensions of Paul's letters.[6] Paul touts these grand ideas about the redeemed people of God, and then urges repentance from the ethical compromises and theological fallacies so misrepresentative of those grand ideas. *This is who you are in Christ* (indicative), *now act like it* (imperative). Paul was as pastorally engaged with the filth and the funk of sinful Christians as any minister who has ever served a church. But his insistence that new creation is on the way and breaking into the present prevented him from becoming a cynic.

2. Struggling with God: Cruciformity and anastasisity. When circumstances seem adverse, we tend to assume that God is closing doors. Alternatively, when Paul saw an open door, he assumed adversity was inevitable: "A wide door for effective work has opened to me, and there are many adversaries" (1 Corinthians 16:9).

Paul's lengthy catalogs of affliction, pain and suffering beg the question, *how did he avoid becoming cynical toward God?*[7]

I think Paul would balk at the disillusionment of most Christian cynics today. He would wonder if we had ever read a page of our New Testaments. Jesus promised his followers a life of adversity, a life Paul knew intimately. There is no way around it—to follow the way of the Christ is to end up on a cross.

But to follow the way of the Christ is also to rise from out of a tomb: "If we have been united with him in a death like his, we shall certainly be united with him in a resurrection like his" (Romans 6:5; cf. Philippians 3:10-11).

In maintaining the dual realities of creation's groaning and eventual renewal, hopeful realism must embrace a life shaped both by the cross (*cruciformity*, Michael Gorman's helpful term for describing the shape of a cross) and by the empty tomb (*anastasisity*, Michael Bird's creative term from the Greek word for "resurrection").[8] Paul had to become content with distress, pain, frustration and suffering because they characterize the mode of life necessary for following the way of the Christ. There is no true Christian ministry apart from the potentially disillusioning experiences of suffering, betrayal and imminent death. These experiences did not lead to cynicism, because Paul knew that the cross is not the terminal stop in following the way of the Christ. Entering Christ's death and agony will result in exiting out of his grave—and one day our own.

When we realize that embracing cross pain and resurrection joy are the biblical standards for discipleship, then our wounds can lead to "newness of life" (Romans 6:4) instead of bitterness of soul. When we realize that "the sufferings of this present time are not worth comparing with the glory that is to be revealed to us" (Romans 8:18), then our trials will become less disillusioning. Hear the perspective of hopeful realism in the following passage as Paul catalogs enormous difficulties alongside traces of resurrection and new creation:

We are afflicted in every way, but not crushed; perplexed, but not driven to despair; persecuted, but not forsaken; struck down, but not destroyed; always carrying in the body the death of Jesus, so that the life of Jesus may also be manifested in our bodies. For we who live are always being given over to death for Jesus' sake, so that the life of Jesus also may be manifested in our mortal flesh. (2 Corinthians 4:8-11)

Why did Paul not become cynical toward God? Because Christ has risen. How could he sing hymns with Silas in the dark of a dungeon? Because Christ has risen. How could he write to the Philippians about joy while serving a prison term? Because Christ has risen. How could he stroll back into Lystra after its citizens had stoned and left him for dead? Because Christ has risen.[9] Paul was not cynical toward God for these miserable circumstances, because he knew they were part of a groaning creation giving way to a new age.

RISING

We had hoped.
   "Where are you two headed?"
   "Emmaus."
   "May I join you?"
The falling sun slowly stretches out the shadows along the road. The conversation is good. For someone who has not been following the news in Jerusalem, the stranger has a lot to say. The mourning disciples realize they do not want to bid him farewell. They are thankful for his interruption. They insist that he join them for supper. Then they see him. They *see* him.
   We hope. Faintly, at times. But we hope. Now and forever. Amen.
   When a dead man interrupts your cynical conversation, something is happening. Something without precedence. When a dead man walks at your side along the road, something is afoot. When the Messiah vacates his tomb, something is stirring. Something new and wild. Something against the establishment. *Death's* establishment. At the voice of the resurrected Lord, the cosmic superstructure of evil de-

tects a virus in the system. A wrench has been tossed into sin's machinery. The foundations start to pop with fissures. It's time to plug up the leak, to contain the fire, to reseal any open tombs. Time for chaos to panic. Time for Satan to go berserk. Resurrection is God shaking his clenched fist in death's face. Resurrection is God whispering death threats in death's ears.

The open tomb of Jesus is a hole in the system that cannot be patched. The re-creating King has climbed up out of his grave. He is out there, loose, at large, roaming free—and returning at dawn.

DISCUSSION QUESTIONS

1. Have you ever experienced the type of deep disappointment and disillusionment with God that led you to say, along with the disciples on the road to Emmaus, "We had hoped . . ."? If so, share the experience.

2. Describe a time when Jesus opened your eyes to see, as he did with Saul, that your previous beliefs and actions were at odds with his mission.

3. What challenges you more about Paul—that he didn't become cynical toward the churches he served *or* that he didn't become cynical toward the God he followed? Explain.

4. How would your life change if you lived in the reality that re-creation and Christ's return are just around the corner?

Notes

Chapter 1: Cynical Between the Edens

[1]The "red pill" and the "matrix" are borrowed from the movie *The Matrix* (1999).

[2]"Cynical," *Merriam-Webster Online* <www.merriam-webster.com/diction ary/cynical>.

[3]Carol V. Hamilton, "Pop Christianity," *OpEdNews.com*, October 17, 2006 <www.opednews.com/articles/2/opedne_carol_ha_061011_pop_christi anity.htm>.

[4]Dietrich Bonhoeffer, *Life Together: The Classic Exploration of Christian Community*, trans. John W. Doberstein (New York: HarperCollins, 1954), pp. 26-27. After writing this chapter, I discovered that Dick Keyes cites from the same Bonhoeffer passage in his *Seeing Through Cynicism: A Reconsideration of the Power of Suspicion* (Downers Grove, Ill.: InterVarsity Press, 2006), p. 203.

Chapter 3: Idealism

[1]Dick Keyes calls the cynic a "closet idealist," building, it seems, on a text he cites from Edmond La B. Cherbonnier who, similarly, dubs the cynic a "covert idealist." See Dick Keyes, *Seeing Through Cynicism: A Reconsideration of the Power of Suspicion* (Downers Grove, Ill.: InterVarsity Press, 2006), pp. 76-77.

[2]For a good taste of the complicated nature of postmodernity (which is too often oversimplified in Christian circles, see the chapter "Vapor's Revenge," in which Peter Leithart provides the story line of postmodernity's messy and tortuous development (Peter J. Leithart, *Solomon Among the Postmoderns* [Grand Rapids: Brazos, 2008], pp. 19-58).

[3]N. T. Wright also likens modernity to the Tower of Babel in his *The Challenge of Jesus: Rediscovering Who Jesus Was and Is* (Downers Grove, Ill.: InterVarsity Press, 1999), pp. 152, 172.

[4]See Richard Bauckham and Trevor Hart, *Hope Against Hope: Christian Eschatology at the Turn of the Millennium* (Grand Rapids: Eerdmans, 1999), particularly chap. 1: "The Decline of Secular Hope."

[5]See N. T. Wright's entire chapter, "Walking to Emmaus in a Postmodern World," in *Challenge of Jesus*, pp. 150-73.

[6]Bauckham and Hart, *Hope Against Hope*, pp. 8-9.

[7]Leithart (see above) dubs postmodernity as "vapor's revenge." He references James

4:14, but his primary texts come from Ecclesiastes (1:2, 12:8). He (convincingly) translates the typical "vanity of vanities" as "vapor of vapors," which better captures *Qoholeth's* emphasis on human transience. See pp. 55, 66-71.

[8]See Mark Ellingsen, *Blessed Are the Cynical: How Original Sin Can Make America a Better Place* (Grand Rapids: Brazos, 2003).

[9]David E. Garland, *Mark*, NIV Application Commentary (Grand Rapids: Zondervan, 1996), p. 61.

[10]I noticed that Eugene Peterson also has a discussion on Elie Wiesel's *Night* in *The Jesus Way: A Conversation on the Ways That Jesus Is the Way* (Grand Rapids: Eerdmans, 2007), pp. 157-60.

[11]François Mauriac (trans. Stella Rodway) in the foreword to Elie Wiesel, *Night* (New York: Avon Books, 1960), p. 10.

[12]REM, "It's the End of the World as We Know It (And I Feel Fine)," *Eponymous*, I.R.S. Records, 1988.

[13]George Eldon Ladd, *A Theology of the New Testament*, ed. Donald A. Hagner, rev. ed. (Grand Rapids: Eerdmans, 1993), pp. 42-46.

Chapter 4: Religiosity

[1]Bill Mallonee, "Skin," *VOL*, Warner Bros., 1996.

[2]Victor Hugo, *Les Misérables*, trans. Lee Fahnestock and Norman MacAfee (New York: Signet Classics, 1987), pp. 1323, 1326.

[3]Eugene Peterson, *Christ Plays in Ten Thousand Places* (Grand Rapids: Eerdmans, 2005), p. 117.

[4]Walter Bauer, *A Greek-English Lexicon of the New Testament and Other Early Christian Literature*, ed. F. Wilbur Gingrich and Frederick W. Danker, 2nd rev. ed. (Chicago: University of Chicago Press, 1979), pp. 603-4.

Chapter 5: Experientialism

[1]Martyn Lloyd-Jones, *Spiritual Depression: Its Causes and Its Cure* (1965; reprint, Grand Rapids: Eerdmans, 2000).

[2]Edith M. Humphrey, *Ecstasy and Intimacy: When the Holy Spirit Meets the Human Spirit* (Grand Rapids: Eerdmans, 2006), p. 203. See her section "When Spirituality Goes Wrong" (pp. 201-21) for a brief overview of contemporary society's fascination with the "spiritual."

[3]For a positive evaluation of emotions in the New Testament, see Matthew A. Elliott, *Faithful Feelings: Rethinking Emotion in the New Testament* (Grand Rapids: Kregel, 2006).

[4]Jonathan Edwards, *A Treatise Concerning Religious Affections in Three Parts*, in *The Works of Jonathan Edwards* 1.2.2 (Carlisle, Penn.: Banner of Truth, 1974), p. 238.

[5]Eugene Peterson, *A Long Obedience in the Same Direction: Discipleship in an Instant Society*, 2nd ed. (Downers Grove, Ill.: InterVarsity Press, 2000), p. 87.

[6]A. W. Tozer, *The Best of A. W. Tozer* (Grand Rapids: Baker, 1978), p. 172.

[7]There is much available on the connections between spirituality and temperaments

or personality types. Since I have already mentioned Lloyd-Jones's book *Spiritual Depression*, I will direct the reader to his discussion on introversion and extroversion on pp. 14-18.

[8]Edwards, "Treatise Concerning Religious Affections" 2.4, p. 249.

[9]See the chapter titled "Are Spiritual Gifts for Today?" in Craig S. Keener, *Gift and Giver: The Holy Spirit for Today* (Grand Rapids: Baker Academic, 2001), pp. 89-112. Keener makes the point that had Paul not had to correct the Corinthians' misconduct at the Lord's Supper (1 Corinthians 11), then we would not know about the practice of the Lord's Supper in Pauline churches (ibid., p. 108)! Well noted, I would say, though the practice of the Lord's Supper is established as normative elsewhere in the Synoptic Gospels.

[10]Rowan Williams, *The Wound of Knowledge: Christian Spirituality from the New Testament to St. John of the Cross*, 2nd rev. ed. (Cambridge, Mass.: Cowley, 1990), p. 182.

[11]It should be noted that God's formation of man in Genesis 2:7 occurs when the divine "breath" enters the dust form of Adam. The Hebrew word for breath here can also be translated "spirit" (see John 20:22). There is also a scene in which Pharaoh hails Joseph as a man "in whom is the Spirit of God" (Genesis 41:38). Bezalel is the first person specifically described by God as filled with the Spirit.

[12]Henri J. M. Nouwen, *The Genesee Diary: Report From a Trappist Monastery* (New York: Doubleday, 1976), pp. 94-95.

[13]See Gordon Fee's brief discussion "The Holy Spirit as Person" in *God's Empowering Presence: The Holy Spirit in the Letters of Paul* (Peabody, Mass.: Hendrickson, 1994), pp. 829-31. See also Keener, *Gift and Giver*, p. 29. For more popular authors who have made this observation, see Francis Chan and Danae Yankoski, *Forgotten God: Reversing Our Tragic Neglect of the Holy Spirit* (Colorado Springs: David C. Cook, 2009), pp. 70, 89; and A. W. Tozer, "How to Be Filled with the Holy Spirit," in *The Best of A. W. Tozer*, ed. Warren Wiersbe (Grand Rapids: Baker, 1978), p. 208.

[14]It is widely recognized, however, that Luke follows more closely the Old Testament tradition in which the Spirit is more understood as a power than a person. Commenting on the presentation of the Spirit in Acts, Jacob Jervell writes, "The Spirit is an impersonal, active force" (Jacob Jervell, *The Theology of the Acts of the Apostles* [New York: Cambridge University Press, 1996], p. 44). Though I would agree that Luke's view of the Spirit is less personal than Paul's or John's view, Luke's pneumatology is intentionally concerned with maintaining continuity with the Old Testament tradition of the Spirit (which is less personal) in order to present Pentecost and its outworkings as the fulfillment of Old Testament eschatological hopes. Scripture's diverse presentation of the Spirit prevents us from depersonalizing the Spirit while yet encouraging our participation in his power and activity. For more on the diverse views on New Testament pneumatology, the best place to start is probably James D. G. Dunn, *Unity and Diversity in the New Testament: An Inquiry into Earliest Christianity* (Philadelphia: Westminster Press, 1977), pp. 174-202.

[15]New Testament scholar James Dunn affirms that "one of Paul's most important con-

tributions to biblical theology" is his presentation of the Holy Spirit as *the Spirit of Christ* (James D. G. Dunn, *The Theology of Paul the Apostle* [Grand Rapids: Eerdmans, 1998], p. 433).

[16]Eugene Peterson, *Christ Plays in Ten Thousand Places* (Grand Rapids: Eerdmans, 2005), p. 61.

[17]See Richard Foster's helpful chapter "Prayer of the Forsaken" in his *Prayer: Finding the Heart's True Home* (San Francisco: HarperSanFrancisco, 1992), pp. 17-25.

[18]Hans Urs von Balthasar, *Prayer*, trans. Graham Harrison (San Francisco: Ignatius Press, 1955), p. 139.

[19]Ibid., pp. 135-36, emphasis added.

[20]The first part of this passage serves as the key exegetical text for Jonathan Edwards's *Treatise Concerning Religious Affections.*

[21]Edwards, *A Treatise Concerning Religious Affections* 1.3.1, p. 243.

[22]Ibid.

Chapter 6: Anti-Intellectualism

[1]Christian Smith with Melinda Lundquist Denton, *Soul Searching: The Religious and Spiritual Lives of American Teenagers* (New York: Oxford University Press, 2005), p. 268.

[2]For a beginner's introduction to the historical development of evangelical anti-intellectualism, I recommend the section "How We Lost Our Minds," in Nancy Pearcey, *Total Truth: Liberating America from Its Cultural Captivity* (Wheaton, Ill.: Crossway, 2005), pp. 251-348. For further study, Mark Noll's work *The Scandal of the Evangelical Mind* (Grand Rapids: Eerdmans, 1994) will be invaluable, along with George Marsden, *Fundamentalism and American Culture: The Shaping of Twentieth-Century Evangelicalism, 1870-1925* (New York: Oxford University Press, 1980). For a secular assessment of evangelical anti-intellectualism, see part two in the Pulitzer Prize–winning book by Richard Hofstadter, *Anti-Intellectualism in America* (New York: Knopf, 1963). In this section I am relying most on my readings in Noll and Pearcey.

[3]For an excellent and readable introduction to Edwards, see George M. Marsden, *A Short Life of Jonathan Edwards* (Grand Rapids: Eerdmans, 2008). Regarding his lack of successors, see Noll, *Scandal of the Evangelical Mind*, p. 24.

[4]Noll, *Scandal of the Evangelical Mind*, pp. 60-64; Iain Murray, *Revival and Revivalism: The Making and Marring of American Evangelicalism, 1750-1858* (Carlisle, Penn.: Banner of Truth, 1994), pp. 163-90.

[5]Pearcey, *Total Truth*, p. 267.

[6]Ibid., pp. 273-79.

[7]Noll, *Scandal of the Evangelical Mind*, pp. 64-67.

[8]Pearcey, *Total Truth*, p. 281.

[9]See Noll's "The Intellectual Disaster of Fundamentalism," in *Scandal of the Evangelical Mind*, pp. 109-45.

[10]Martin E. Marty, introduction to Helmut Thielicke, *A Little Exercise for Young Theologians*, trans. Charles L. Taylor (Grand Rapids: Eerdmans, 1962), p. xiii.

[11]Thielicke, *A Little Exercise for Young Theologians*, p. 10.

[12]Ibid., pp. 11-12 (emphasis added).

[13]Ibid., p. 17.

[14]The Hebrew text is translated "heart," "soul" and "might" (or "strength" [NIV]). It is interesting that Jesus specifically adds "mind" in his recitation of the passage. Loving God with the mind is clearly in view in the Hebrew, but an audience influenced by the Hellenistic divisions between body, soul and mind would have likely benefited from Jesus' specific reference.

Chapter 7: Cultural Irrelevance

[1]David Kinnaman and Gabe Lyons, *unChristian: What a New Generation Really Thinks About Christianity . . . and Why It Matters* (Grand Rapids: Baker, 2007), pp. 121-52.

[2]Ibid., p. 219.

[3]After writing this chapter, I noticed that there is a book out called *Mere Churchianity*. See Michael Spencer, *Mere Churchianity: Finding Your Way Back to Jesus-Shaped Spirituality* (Colorado Springs: Waterbrook Press, 2010).

[4]I am grateful for my friend Pete Bradburn who instantly provided me with these marquee messages from his extensive collection!

[5]Earl Crepps, *Reverse Mentoring: How Young Leaders Can Transform the Church and Why We Should Let Them* (San Francisco: Jossey-Bass, 2008).

[6]*Irreverent* was apparently taken from an endorsement by Robert Lanham for Jason Boyett's Pocket Guide series published by Jossey-Bass.

[7]Kinnaman and Lyons, *unChristian*, p. 126.

[8]The Greek word *anōthen* can be interpreted "born from above" or "born again" or both! See the ESV note on this word.

[9]John Stott, "A Call to Radical Discipleship," quoted in Kinnaman and Lyons, *unChristian*, p. 151.

[10]See "From Relevance to Prayer," in Henri Nouwen, *In the Name of Jesus: Reflections on Christian Leadership* (New York: Crossroad, 1989), pp. 13-32.

[11]Henri Nouwen, *In the Name of Jesus*, p. 17.

Chapter 8: The Way of the Prophet

[1]William S. Lasor et al., *Old Testament Survey: The Message, Form, and Background of the Old Testament*, 2nd ed. (Grand Rapids: Eerdmans, 1996), p. 388.

[2]Abraham J. Heschel, *The Prophets* (New York: Harper & Row, 1962), p. 52.

[3]Walter Brueggemann, *The Prophetic Imagination*, 2nd ed. (Minneapolis: Fortress, 2001), p. 81.

[4]I am thankful to Dr. Mark Gignilliat at Beeson Divinity School for suggesting I mention the scene in Jeremiah 20.

[5]Brueggemann, *Prophetic Imagination*, p. 99.

[6]See Brueggemann's chapter "Prophetic Energizing and the Emergence of Amazement," in ibid., pp. 59-79.

Chapter 9: The Way of the Sage

[1]Though there were clearly men and women who functioned as "religious specialists" in the capacities of prophets, priests and sages, these roles often overlapped and were not clearly defined. See Lester L. Grabbe's article "Prophets, Priests, Diviners and Sages in Ancient Israel," in *Of Prophets' Visions and the Wisdom of Sages*, JSOTSupp 162, ed. Heather A. McKay and David J. A. Clines (Sheffield, U.K.: Sheffield Academic Press, 1993), pp. 43-62.

[2]There are no conclusive lists of these psalms, but one Old Testament introduction lists Psalms 1; 32; 34; 37; 49; 73; 112; 127–28; and 133. See William S. Lasor et al., *Old Testament Survey*, 2nd ed. (Grand Rapids: Eerdmans, 1996), p. 459; see also p. 440.

[3]W. H. Bellinger Jr., *The Testimony of Poets and Sages: The Psalms and Wisdom Literature* (Macon, Ga.: Smyth & Helwys, 1998), p. 54.

[4]Dick Keyes makes similar observations about the parallels between modern-day cynics and the "scoffer" of the wisdom literature. See Richard Keyes, *Seeing Through Cynicism* (Downers Grove, Ill.: InterVarsity Press, 2006), p. 162.

[5]Daniel J. Estes, *Handbook on the Wisdom Books and Psalms* (Grand Rapids: Baker Academic, 2005), p. 219.

[6]Bellinger, *Testimony of Poets and Sages*, p. 57; see also p. 77.

[7]William S. Lasor et al., *Old Testament Survey: The Message, Form and Background of the Old Testament,* 2nd ed. (Grand Rapids: Eerdmans, 1996), p. 495.

[8]David F. Ford, *Christian Wisdom: Desiring God and Learning in His Love*, Cambridge Studies in Christian Doctrine (New York: Cambridge University Press, 2007), pp. 126-27.

[9]Richard J. Clifford, "Introduction to Wisdom Literature," in *The New Interpreter's Bible* (Nashville: Abingdon, 1997), 5:11.

[10]Lasor et al., *Old Testament Survey,* pp. 493-94.

[11]See Corrine L. Patton, "The Beauty of the Beast: Leviathan and Behemoth in Light of Catholic Theology," in *The Whirlwind: Essays on Job, Hermeneutics and Theology in Memory of Jane Morse*, JSOTSup 336, ed. Stephen L. Cook, Corinne L. Patton, and James W. Watts (New York: Sheffield Academic Press, 2001), pp. 142-67.

[12]J. Gerald Janzen, *Job*, Interpretation Commentaries, ed. James L. Mays, Patrick D. Miller and Paul J. Achtemeier (Atlanta: John Knox Press, 1985), p. 246.

[13]Estes, *Handbook on the Wisdom Books*, p. 30.

[14]Qoholeth as cynic: "To modern sensibilities, the book may seem shockingly pessimistic and even nihilistic. It reminds us that ancient wisdom literature had a bleak and cynical strain" (Richard J. Clifford, *The Wisdom Literature*, Interpreting Biblical Texts [Nashville: Abingdon, 1998], pp. 97-98). James Crenshaw would probably have no problem calling Qoholeth a cynic. See James L. Crenshaw, *Old Testament Wisdom: An Introduction* (Louisville, Ky.: Westminster John Knox, 1998), pp. 116-39. Qoholeth as not a cynic: "Ecclesiastes is a commentary on the meaning of life, and its thesis is that human existence is like 'mist.' Hardly cynical, Ecclesiastes considers life from a realist point of view" (Robert W. Wall, *Community of the Wise:*

The Letter of James, New Testament in Context, ed. Howard Clark Lee and J. Andrew Overman [Valley Forge, Penn.: Trinity Press International, 1997], p. 220).

[15]W. Sibley Towner, "Ecclesiastes," in *The New Interpreter's Bible* (Nashville: Abingdon, 1997), 5:267-68.

[16]Though it should be noted that Crenshaw believes Qoholeth "pronounces judgment on God" for the disappointments at the end of the quest for wisdom mentioned in Ecclesiastes 1:13 (Crenshaw, *Old Testament Wisdom*, p. 116). Hesitantly and respectfully, I think this assessment is unnecessarily rash.

[17]Peter J. Leithart, *Solomon Among the Postmoderns* (Grand Rapids: Brazos, 2008), p. 163.

[18]Ibid.

[19]J. I. Packer, *Knowing God*, 20th anniversary ed. (Downers Grove, Ill.: InterVarsity Press, 1973), p. 106. I am thankful to Dr. Adam McCollum for referencing Packer's comments on Ecclesiastes in a biblical Hebrew course at Beeson Divinity School.

[20]Lasor et al., *Old Testament Survey,* pp. 500, 509.

[21]Ibid., p. 509.

Chapter 10: The Way of the Tragic Poet

[1]William S. Lasor et al., *Old Testament Survey: The Message, Form and Background of the Old Testament,* 2nd ed. (Grand Rapids: Eerdmans, 1996), p. 430.

[2]REM, "Shiny Happy People," *Out of Time*, Warner Brothers Records, 1991.

[3]Walter Brueggemann, *Spirituality of the Psalms* (Minneapolis: Fortress, 2002), p. xii.

[4]Claus Westermann, *Praise and Lament in the Psalms*, trans. Keith R. Crim and Richard N. Soulen (Atlanta: John Knox Press, 1981), p. 267.

[5]See "The Paradox of the Psalms," in Kathleen Norris, *The Cloister Walk* (New York: Riverhead, 1987), pp. 90-107.

[6]Bill Mallonee, "You Were the Only Girl for Me," *Friendly Fire*, Fundamental Records, 2005.

[7]Bernard W. Anderson with Steven Bishop, *Out of the Depths: The Psalms Speak for Us Today*, 3rd ed. (Louisville, Ky.: Westminster John Knox, 2000), p. 51.

[8]John Eaton, *The Psalms: A Historical and Spiritual Commentary with an Introduction and New Translation* (New York: Continuum, 2005), p. 28.

[9]Daniel J. Estes, *Handbook on the Wisdom Books and Psalms* (Grand Rapids: Baker Academic, 2005), pp. 165-66.

[10]Eugene Peterson, *A Long Obedience in the Same Direction: Discipleship in an Instant Society* (Downers Grove, Ill.: InterVarsity Press, 2000), p. 75, emphasis added.

[11]Brevard S. Childs, *Biblical Theology of the Old and New Testaments: Theological Reflection on the Christian Bible* (Minneapolis: Fortress, 1992), p. 192, emphasis added.

[12]Westermann, *Praise and Lament in the Psalms*, p. 266.

[13]Brueggemann, *Spirituality of the Psalms*, p. xiii.

[14]Thomas Merton, *Praying the Psalms* (Collegeville, Minn.: Liturgical Press, 1956), p. 35.

[15]In Jeremiah 12:5, God responds to one of Jeremiah's lamenting prayers with questions: "If you have raced with men on foot, and they have wearied you, how will you compete with horses? And if in a safe land you are so trusting, what will you do in the thicket of the Jordan?" (see also Jeremiah 15:1-9). For a favorable answer to strong questions, see Jeremiah 15:19-21.

[16]David Dark, *The Sacredness of Questioning Everything* (Grand Rapids: Zondervan, 2009), p. 153.

[17]Richard Foster, *Prayer: Finding the Heart's True Home* (San Francisco: HarperSanFrancisco, 1992), p. 23.

[18]There are eight imprecatory psalms in which this imprecatory language is found most densely (Psalms 7; 35; 58; 59; 69; 83; 109; 137). See Estes, *Handbook on the Wisdom Books and Psalms*, p. 172.

[19]John Goldingay, *Psalms*, Baker Commentary on the Old Testament, Wisdom and Psalms, ed. Tremper Longman III (Grand Rapids: Baker Academic, 2006), 1:66-67.

[20]Anderson, *Out of the Depths*, p. 71.

[21]Walter Brueggemann, *The Message of the Psalms* (Minneapolis: Augsburg Press, 1984), p. 77, cited in Goldingay, *Psalms*, p. 67.

[22]See Kyu Nam Jung, "Prayer in the Psalms," in *Teach Us to Pray: Prayer in the Bible and the World*, ed. D. A. Carson (Grand Rapids: Baker, 1990), pp. 50-52.

[23]See Psalms 82, 90 and 123, though none equals the joylessness of Psalm 88.

Chapter 11: The Way of the Christ

[1]See N. T. Wright, *The Challenge of Jesus: Rediscovering Who Jesus Was and Is* (Downers Grove, Ill.: InterVarsity Press, 1999), p. 11. See also Scot McKnight, "The Jesus We'll Never Know," *Christianity Today*, April 2010, p. 23. As a professor of New Testament, McKnight gives a "standardized psychological test" in his course on Jesus that asks students questions regarding their understanding of Jesus and then asks about their understanding of themselves. The results overwhelmingly demonstrate that we envision Jesus to be like ourselves.

[2]Craig A. Evans, *Fabricating Jesus: How Modern Scholars Distort the Gospels* (Downers Grove, Ill.: InterVarsity Press, 2006), p. 100.

[3]See Gregory A. Boyd, *Cynic, Sage, or Son of God* (Wheaton, Ill.: Victor Books, 1995), pp. 10-12. For a list of the books associating Jesus with Greco-Roman Cynicism, see the sources cited in Ben Witherington III, *Jesus the Sage: The Pilgrimage of Wisdom* (Minneapolis: Fortress, 1994), p. 123 n. 16: F. Gerald Downing, *Christ and the Cynics: Jesus and Other Radicals in First Century Traditions* (Sheffield, U.K.: JSOT Press, 1988), and *Jesus and the Threat of Freedom* (London: SCM Press, 1987); John Dominic Crossan, *The Historical Jesus: The Life of a Mediterranean Jewish Peasant* (San Francisco: HarperSanFrancisco, 1991); Burton Mack, *A Myth of Innocence* (Philadelphia: Fortress, 1988).

[4]After writing this chapter I later read Dick Keyes's *Seeing Through Cynicism* (Downers Grove, Ill.: InterVarsity Press, 2006), in which he addresses the claims of Jesus as a Cynic in the opening of his chapter "What If the Transcendent Has Come to

Earth?" (pp. 134-44). I appreciate the way he expresses his own assessment that many historical Jesus scholars have simply reconstructed Jesus in their own image: "Jesus became an incarnation of their own values, his story a projection of their idealized autobiography" (p. 138).

[5]Along with Boyd, see "Alien Contexts: The Case Against Jesus as a Cynic," in Evans, *Fabricating Jesus*, pp. 100-122; and Witherington's chapter "Hokmah Meets Sophia: Jesus the Cynic?" in *Jesus the Sage*, pp. 117-45. Evans cites these works in n. 9 from "Alien Contexts": David E. Aune, "Jesus and Cynics in First-Century Palestine: Some Critical Considerations," in *Hillel and Jesus*, ed. James Charlesworth and Loren L. Johns (Minneapolis: Fortress, 1997), pp. 176-92; Hans Dieter Betz, "Jesus and the Cynics: Survey and Analysis of a Hypothesis," *The Journal of Religion* 74 (1994): 453-75; Christopher M. Tuckett, "A Cynic Q?" *Biblica* 70 (1989): 349-76; and *Q and the History of Early Christianity* (Edinburgh: T & T Clark, 1996), pp. 368-91.

[6]Jürgen Moltmann, *The Crucified God: The Cross of Christ as the Foundation and Criticism of Christian Theology* (New York: Harper & Row, 1974), p. 152.

[7]See "Wisdom in Person: Jesus the Sage," in Witherington, *Jesus the Sage*, pp. 147-208.

[8]Joel B. Green, *The Gospel of Luke*, New International Commentary on the New Testament (Grand Rapids: Eerdmans, 1997), p. 266.

[9]W. D. Davies and Dale C. Allison, *Matthew*, ed. Dale C. Allison (New York: T & T Clark, 2004), p. 413.

[10]Claus Westermann, *Praise and Lament in the Psalms*, trans. Keith R. Crim and Richard N. Soulen (Atlanta: John Knox Press, 1981), pp. 264-65.

[11]Moltmann, *Crucified God*, p. 152.

[12]See Joel Marcus's brilliant and careful treatment of the cry of dereliction in his essay "Identity and Ambiguity in Markan Christology," in *Seeking the Identity of Jesus: A Pilgrimage*, ed. Beverly Roberts Gaventa and Richard B. Hays (Grand Rapids: Eerdmans, 2008), pp.133-47, esp. 140-47.

[13]Jason Byassee has provided a helpful presentation of St. Augustine's understanding of Jesus' use of laments in *Praise Seeking Understanding: Reading the Psalms with Augustine* (Grand Rapids: Eerdmans, 2007), see esp. pp. 156-67.

[14]Joel Marcus, *The Way of the Lord: Christological Exegesis of the Old Testament in the Gospel of Mark* (Louisville, Ky.: Westminster John Knox, 1992), pp. 172-86.

Chapter 12: On the Roads to Emmaus and Damascus

[1]There is a distinction between apocalypticism and eschatology in biblical scholarship, but I am using the latter term in order to avoid confusion for readers less familiar with the technical parlance.

[2]For a helpful overview of these elements, see David E. Aune, "Apocalypticism," in *Dictionary of Paul and His Letters*, ed. Gerald F. Hawthorne, Ralph P. Martin and Daniel G. Reid (Downers Grove, Ill.: InterVarsity Press, 1993), pp. 25-35.

[3]I know of no better resource for exploring these ideas than N. T. Wright, *The Resur-*

rection of the Son of God, Christian Origins and the Question of God 3 (Minneapolis: Fortress, 2003).

[4]These sketches are loosely adapted from George Eldon Ladd, *A Theology of the New Testament*, ed. Donald A. Hagner, rev. ed. (Grand Rapids: Eerdmans, 1993), pp. 66-67.

[5]Michael Gorman, "A Summary of the Theology of 1 Corinthians," *Cross Talk*, July 29, 2008 <www.michaeljgorman.net/2008/07/29/a-summary-of-the-theology-of-1-corinthians>.

[6]These are common terms used to described Paul's basis and mode of ethical exhortation. See James D. G. Dunn, *The Theology of Paul the Apostle* (Grand Rapids: Eerdmans, 1998), pp. 626-31.

[7]Paul certainly does not wear the garb of a contemporary cynic, but these catalogs of trials share some common threads with the writings of Greco-Roman Cynics and Stoics. See Moyer V. Hubbard, *Christianity in the Greco-Roman World: A Narrative Introduction* (Peabody, Mass.: Hendrickson, 2010), p. 100 (see also pp. 101-2). For a closer look at Paul's possible affinities with Greco-Roman Cynicism, see Abraham J. Malherbe, *Paul and the Popular Philosophers* (Minneapolis: Fortress Press, 1989); and F. Gerald Downing, *Cynics, Paul and the Pauline Churches: Cynics and Christian Origins II* (New York: Routledge, 1998).

[8]Michael J. Gorman, *Cruciformity: Paul's Narrative Spirituality of the Cross* (Grand Rapids: Eerdmans, 2001). Michael F. Bird, *Introducing Paul: The Man, His Mission and His Message* (Downers Grove, Ill.: InterVarsity Press, 2008), pp. 162-68.

[9]I am thankful for a sermon I heard by Joel Busby on April 7, 2010, titled "The Hope of the Resurrection," which inspired this paragraph.

Acknowledgments

I am deeply grateful . . .

For those who read portions of this book along the way: Lauren Winner, John Utz, Scott Ryan, Mark Gignilliat, Tammy H., Wayne Coppins, Austin Campbell, Rob O'Callaghan, and Joel Busby.

For the guy who gave me a chance to write a book: Dave Zimmerman with Likewise Books.

For those who provided great contexts for the writing: Bill Mallonee and Muriah Rose (for the most lyrical music out there) and the guys at Primavera Coffee (for giving me great coffee along with a table and chair).

For the travel companions on that 1997 journey: Passengers O'Callaghan, Koo and Sims.

For co-laborers in ministry: Tracy, Teresa, Jim, the Crossroads World-wide community and Broad River Community Church (Boiling Springs, N.C.); the deacons at Mount Hermon Community Church (Durham, N.C.); Joel, Sarah, Connie, and the pastors, staff and elders at Mountain Brook Community Church (Birmingham, Ala.).

For my mentors during seminary: Wallace Williams, Robert Smith, Mike Melton, Bruce Winter and Norfleete Day (while at Beeson); Kavin Rowe, Joel Marcus and Richard Hays (while at Duke).

For those who allowed me in their lives as a pastor: the students at Gardner-Webb University (2002-2006); the dear church family at Mount Hermon (2006-2008); and the students in the UCF community (2008-2011).

For Betty and Ed Darnell for allowing Miranda and I to share their pain . . . and joy. This book is in memory of Pamela.

For four, sweet little people who have had to be so patient with their dad: Brynn, Hayden, Cavan, and Adalyn.

And I am so thankful for my wife, Miranda, to whom this book is dedicated. She is the most godly person I know . . . and still beyond all dreaming. Most importantly, I am thankful for the One who is the Highest and the Best . . . the One who is, who was and who is to come.

LIKEWISE. *Go and do.*

A man comes across an ancient enemy, beaten and left for dead. He lifts the wounded man onto the back of a donkey and takes him to an inn to tend to the man's recovery. Jesus tells this story and instructs those who are listening to "go and do likewise."

Likewise books explore a compassionate, active faith lived out in real time. When we're skeptical about the status quo, Likewise books challenge us to create culture responsibly. When we're confused about who we are and what we're supposed to be doing, Likewise books help us listen for God's voice. When we're discouraged by the troubled world we've inherited, Likewise books encourage us to hold onto hope.

In this life we will face challenges that demand our response. Likewise books face those challenges with us so we can act on faith.

likewisebooks.com